I PUT MY SWORD AWAY

Yacoub Yousif

I PUT MY SWORD AWAY

An Iraqi Soldier's Journey from
Battlefield to Brotherhood

Bruderhof

Published by the Bruderhof
Rifton, New York, USA
Robertsbridge, East Sussex, UK
Elsmore, NSW, Australia

ISBN 978-0-87486-710-7

CONTENTS

Prologue 1

1 Growing Up 7

2 Iraqi Life and Culture 14

3 Schooling 17

4 Iraq at War 22

5 Detention 27

6 To the Battlefield 34

7 Waking to Reality 39

8 From Death to Life 46

9 Why War? 55

10 I Can Die but I Cannot Kill 64

11 A Way Out 68

12 Finding a Partner 74

13 Layla 81

14 No More War 85

15 Marriage 88

16 Mariam 93

17 Let Me Out! 97

18 Complications 103

19 Agitation on the Home Front 109
20 A Worldwide Search 116
21 Iraqi Airlines, Here We Come 121
22 Refugees 126
23 Church Life 131
24 What Is Church? 134
25 Coming to Clarity 141
26 Seeking Community 146
27 A New Beginning 153
28 Eberhard 159
29 Reflection 163
    Epilogue 167
    Family Album 171

PROLOGUE

Amer waved his arms frantically as he ran toward me.

"Yacoub," he shouted. "The general wants you to go with him to the front!"

Usually soft-spoken, Amer was now out of breath as he hurried to my side.

"To the front? But I just this minute got back from furlough!"

"No matter, we've only got five minutes. Come on, hurry up!"

Short, stocky Amer, with his deep brown skin, was the general's driver, and I was one of his bodyguards.

The general expected his bodyguards to look sharp at all times, so I didn't dare appear without shaving. I scraped a razor across my chin in record time—without a mirror!—put on my army boots and helmet and ran to the arms depot to check out my folding-stock Kalashnikov and ammunition vest. Then I rushed outside to the Range Rover.

Our supervisor, Ibrahim, and three other bodyguards were waiting.

"*Ayamak Sa'ida*, Yacoub," they greeted me quietly. "How was your holiday furlough?"

"I had a great time, thanks." Looking around, I added, "But where is our platoon leader—where is Second Lieutenant Abdul Razak?"

Silence.

I looked around at the faces of my comrades. "What's the matter?" I asked, bewildered.

Finally, Salah replied, "He was injured."

"Injured? How did it happen?"

"That's not the worst of it. Ali was also hit. He...he's..."

"What?" I exclaimed. "What happened to him?"

They looked down at their boots. "He's dead. He's a martyr."

I was stunned. Ali dead? I couldn't believe it.

"How did it..."

"Not now, be quiet. The general is coming." We all looked in the direction of headquarters.

Brigadier General Qais was the commander of the Fifteenth Division—the Al-Farouk Troops of the Seventh Corps. As he strode up, we all saluted him. His light skin contrasted with his olive green uniform. The epaulettes on his shoulders—a falcon insignia above three stars— made his square frame seem even stockier. His thin moustache gave him a serious look.

We all climbed into the Range Rover, Ibrahim next to Amer in front and us four bodyguards all the way in the back. General Qais climbed onto the seat behind the driver.

Gunning the engine, Amer dropped into first gear and lurched forward. We were on our way to the front.

Oh God, Ali is gone! I wanted to ask my comrades how it had happened, but could barely speak as we bumped along toward the front.

We saw explosions on all sides as we neared the fighting. The road became rough and pitted, so Amer slowed down. "Sir, the road ahead is being bombed. Shall I take a detour?" he asked.

"No, just carry on."

The noise of bombs suddenly bursting around us was so deafening I couldn't question him further. "God!" I whispered to myself, "Are we really going to keep going on this dangerous road? Allah help us."

There was a brief lull in the bombing, so I leaned over to Salah and asked, "Where are we going?"

"To the Om Al-Rasas Islands," he answered. The two Om Al-Rasas Islands were located in the Shatt al-Arab River in southern Iraq—between Iraq and Iran.

A picture of Layla flashed through my mind just then. I had had a wonderful furlough in Baghdad and was able to see her several times. I loved her and already missed her, even though I had seen her just hours before. I wondered when we would ever be able to get married. With the offensive going the way it was, who knew when the general might let me go on furlough again. Would I even live that long?

There was a constant sound of bullets zinging through the shattered date-palm orchard through which we were passing. We all jumped as a bomb tore up the ground beside the road with an ear-splitting blast. The vehicle swerved but then steadied.

A bit further on, Amer brought the Range Rover to a sudden stop. The bombing and shooting were still going on, but there was nothing we could do about it. We were forced to walk out in the open, without any protection, as we escorted the general. Two of us walked in front of him and two behind. Ibrahim, along with Amer, waited by the Range Rover.

The island was in shambles after the attacks and counter-attacks. Orchards were reduced to pulp, gravel roads were pitted with craters. As we walked through the frontline trenches, there were deep layers of shrapnel that crunched as we shuffled our feet through the debris on the ground.

Finally, we came to a bunker and dove into the relative safety of its walls.

The bunker had a steel-reinforced concrete roof covered with sandbags, on top of which was a two-foot layer of soil. We continued to watch the bombing through an observation slit in the bunker wall. While the general was talking on his radio, I saw four Iraqi soldiers, bullets whizzing around them, carrying a dead comrade on a blanket back behind the front line.

It was much quieter in the bunker, so I turned to Salah and asked, "Tell me, what happened to Ali?"

"Well," he began, "you know that the special forces Sixty-Sixth Brigade was deployed to retake the island..."

"Retake the island...?" I ventured.

"Yes, didn't you know? The Iranians attacked the Om Al-Rasas Islands while you were gone. You're lucky you were on furlough. They sent frogmen and speedboats up Iran's Karun River and overran the first of the two islands after midnight the day before Christmas.

"So we were holding one of the islands, while the Iranians held the other one. General Qais ordered Colonel Bareq and his men to rush the bridge between the two, but it was madness—certain death if they did. The Iranians were firing point-blank at them. So the men refused to obey the colonel's order."

"Are they crazy?" I exclaimed. "They'll be executed for refusing to obey!"

"Yeah, I know. But when General Qais heard about it, he ordered Colonel Bareq to get out. That was a real humiliation. You know, Bareq was awarded the Medal of Courage *three times*. Nobody questions *his* courage.

"Then General Qais commanded *us* to storm the bridge, which we did. We lost a lot of men, but most of the Iranians were killed. In the end, we were able to take back the island."

Is that when Abdul Razak was injured?" I asked.

"Yes, and also when Ali was killed."

We were quiet for a moment, thinking of our lost comrade.

"Anyway," Salah continued, "General Qais wants to

check that everything is under control. But now is the most dangerous time. The Iranians are going crazy, shooting and bombing out of revenge."

While we were speaking, an 80-millimeter mortar shell made a direct hit on our bunker. The noise inside was deafening and the blast nearly knocked us off our feet.

With our ears ringing, we watched in horror as cracks laced through the concrete above our heads. We held our breath, waiting for the roof to cave in. At that moment, another bomb fell right in front of the bunker, just as I was turning to one side. A piece of shrapnel spiraled in, barely missing me. It hit Salah squarely in the chest.

Paralyzed with fear, I was sure I was going to die. Whatever was I doing here? I had been brought up in such a protected environment. How had I been sucked into this hellhole?

I

GROWING UP

I was born on Wednesday, June 18, 1958, in the Sinnak district in the center of Baghdad, the capital of my beloved homeland, Iraq. A month after my birth, the July Fourteenth Revolution—a bloody military coup—took place, ending the monarchy and ushering in the republic. My family tells me that at the sound of the bombings I turned my head from one side to the other. So it seems that from my earliest days I was affected by the unrest in my country.

My family was nominally Christian, but not devout. I had one younger brother named Raad. My parent's marriage had been arranged, and since it was not their choice, they never found a way to adjust to each other. When I was two years old they divorced. I remained in Baghdad with Baba, my father Yousif, while Raad moved to Mosul with Mama, Kawkab, to live with my maternal grandparents.

I was devastated, and as a result of the divorce I had a very difficult childhood. I missed my mother terribly, although my grandmother Najma, whom we called Nana, lived with us and helped to care for me. Nana had a tough life, because my grandfather died when Baba was only six months old and my Aunt Victoria only five. Nana never remarried and had to raise the children on her own.

She was short with fair skin, dark black hair, and dark green eyes—like me. She was a nurse, and during the sixties she worked in a medical clinic in the Al-Thawra district and had to wear an *abaa*—a veil—when she was traveling back and forth to work, but not at home, while shopping, or at the clinic. Because she didn't wear the veil, many people in our neighborhood thought she was Jewish. She loved me very much and brought me up.

Mama's family and Baba's family were constantly feuding and, unfortunately, I was caught in the middle. This bickering went on throughout my entire childhood. Once, when I was about four years old, I went to visit Mama and her family. I could feel animosity toward me, because I "belonged to the other side." After that, I was not usually allowed to go there.

There were times when the family feud became violent. I was out riding in the car with Baba one day, sitting in the back seat watching the streets go by, when all of a sudden one of Mama's relatives flagged us down, getting Baba to stop the car. The man approached the car and, without warning, opened the door and started beating Baba with his fists. Baba reached down to get a metal club from under his seat in order to defend himself, but the assailant was already walking away.

Baba loved me very much, but he sometimes displayed a certain lack of sensitivity. For instance, once we had to go to the train station. While he was carrying me, he jokingly announced, "Child for sale!" I felt insecure and vulnerable and was deeply wounded.

Nevertheless, he doted on me, spoiling me with the best toys and clothes, as well as a cat and several dogs. He sent me to the best schools in Baghdad. He was of average height, with a slight build and receding hairline. He had an olive complexion, a round face, and full lips. His lively personality was infectious, and he was often laughing and joking.

Baba was not religious and was not raised with Christian values, even though he called himself a Christian. He was very energetic—up at five o'clock every morning—and had a practical bent.

When I was ten years old he married Julie, one of Mama's cousins. Unfortunately, Nana had to move to her own house because she and Julie didn't get along. Soon after their marriage my brother, Arkan, was born. Six years later I also received a little sister named Hind.

In spite of the problems, there was one aspect of family life that helped compensate for the problems. Baba loved music and played the violin and piano. Our home was always filled with music and musical instruments–trombone, trumpet, Arabic drum, keyboard, banjo, and guitar.

Although I basked in this atmosphere, I didn't start making music myself until I was in my teens. At that time, I begged Baba to buy me a drum kit. "Not until you finish high school–and with high grades!" he insisted. So I had to practice on a drum kit of pots and pans and lids. I also began to improvise on the keyboard, as well as recorder, banjo, and guitar. My friends and I would get together for jam sessions. Later, when I was in the Al-Jamhoria High School in the Al-Mu'alemin district of Baghdad, I played Arabic drum in the school band, which often performed at school events. One of the members of our band, my friend Raad, sang very well and sounded exactly like Abdel Halim Hafez, a famous Egyptian singer.

Like boys everywhere, I loved sports: soccer, basketball, table tennis, and bodybuilding. I was on my class soccer team in high school and in university played basketball on a departmental team.

In addition to the usual family celebrations and outings, we often went to public swimming pools and enjoyed the public parks and playgrounds.

Since Iraqis are warm and hospitable, with strong family ties and close-knit neighborhoods, it was not unusual for us to drop in on each other unannounced. Regardless of ethnic or religious affiliation, we lived harmoniously–in fact, with a great sense of humor.

Neighborhood children played soccer, flew kites,

played with marbles and spinning top, and raised pigeons together. During Ramadan the young people of the neighborhood would spend the beautiful evenings together, after the Muslims broke the fast, socializing and playing games in the streets for most of the night.

Also during Ramadan younger children would roam the streets of the neighborhood, knocking on doors and singing *Majeena, Ya Majeena* in hopes of getting some candy. Sometimes children and adults from two different neighborhoods would play a game called Mheibes or Bat against each other. In this game, similar to "Up Jenkins," one team would hide a ring and the other team would look for it. The losing team had to buy a full tray of Baklava pastry for both teams to share!

In summer we spent our annual holidays in the beautiful tourist areas of Kurdistan, northern Iraq, or Lebanon.

One of the nicest spots was the village of Sarsank near Mosul in the north of Iraq. We stayed in a first-class hotel that had a swimming pool and restaurant. In the evenings a band played in a garden by the pool while people danced. We often took our maid along with us on these trips. We did a lot of hiking in this verdant, mountainous region that was dotted with orchards.

Once we drove to the nearby town of Amadiya–a whole town on top of a flat mountain–traveling with another family. Fareed, the father of this family, was hesitant to drive up the mountain because it was so steep.

"What if a tire blows out suddenly on that steep mountain and we fall over the cliff?" he said nervously.

"You don't need to worry," we assured him. "Just follow us; we have driven this road before."

Much to his surprise, he made it up and back without falling into the abyss.

We traveled to Lebanon almost every year, and these trips were wonderful. Aunt Victoria, who had married a Lebanese man, lived there with her family. Her family lived–and still lives–in Beirut, but they used to spend the summer up in the mountains in places like the village of Beskinta–a village so pretty it seemed like paradise on earth. It was full of cherry, peach, plum, and apple orchards, and was renowned for its spring water. It was also located on a mountain, and looked out over the vast valley flanked by mountains that were snow-peaked year round, especially the famous Mount Sannine. Moreover, the people of the village had an engaging culture, with spontaneous visits to each other's homes. Various events were held there, such as singing evenings and volleyball matches.

We young people enjoyed hiking on the wooded mountains. During our hikes we picked pine cones and ate the seeds inside. We also picked wild almonds from the trees in the forest and made fires with dead twigs to barbeque the potatoes we had brought along. The mountains were so steep that I once lost my footing and rolled all the way down a slope, stopping just short of a busy street! Sometimes, as we passed through the woods, we would stop at the old, stony Chapel of Saint Thecla just off our footpath and sit reverently for a few minutes' rest.

2

IRAQI LIFE AND CULTURE

In many ways we are molded by both the good and bad aspects of our environment so, like peoples everywhere, our culture brought out both the best and the worst in people. On the one hand there was a warm, simple, friendly relationship among neighbors, without religious or sectarian discrimination, while on the other hand society was peppered with petty social ills—white lies, gossip, grudges, class distinctions, and immorality. We were also plagued with serious inequalities, like restricted religious liberty and limited women's rights, not to mention outright barbarism in the tribal regions.

There were many tribal groups, and although their culture had positive aspects, they also had a sinister side. They exhibited strong solidarity and mutual assistance, but they also were prone to vendettas and revenge—often leading to reprisals. It was frequently necessary to send a delegation to negotiate some sort of settlement.

For instance, while in the army my brother was sent to prison when he accidentally killed a fellow soldier. He had backed up a tank during a training session and ran over one of his comrades, leading to a situation that could have exploded into a major family feud.

"This guy's family is going to get you!" his sergeant warned him.

"But what can I do?"

The sergeant thought for a moment, and said, " See if the commanding officer will let you out of prison for a while, so you can go talk to the family–I don't know, offer them money, or something."

"But I don't dare go there. I don't know how to deal with a situation like this."

"Okay, I'll tell you what. Don't worry, I know these people and I'll come with you. Go home and get, maybe, a thousand dinars–that should be enough. Then we'll go together."

In the end the family accepted the *fas'l*–the settlement–and all was forgiven. After putting in a six-month prison sentence my brother was freed. But in other cases such an incident might lead to revenge killing, with reprisals back and forth until someone finally came up with a *fas'l* that was acceptable.

Despite these problems, there were many religious, God-fearing people who longed to do what is right, whatever their religion. There was a tangible sense of community and brotherliness. For instance, when we

moved into our new house in the Baghdad Al-Jadeeda*
district of Baghdad in 1968, neighbors who didn't even
know us brought us three meals a day for three days.
There was an innocence and kindness in society that is
increasingly rare today, even in the Middle East.

Iraq was probably the most advanced country in the
region during the 1980s and 90s, with flourishing tractor,
cement, phosphate, pharmaceutical, and canned food
industries. There was an enormous need to improve the
country's infrastructure, and that was being funded by
the nationalized oil industry. National health insurance
covered all medical and dental care, and education was
free at all levels up to and including university. Moreover,
the government funded sports, the arts, and Iraqi culture.
Crime was low; we could travel anywhere in the country
and feel completely safe day and night.

On the other hand, trade was centralized and not
free. The Iraqi government was a single-party state and
had zero tolerance toward any kind of dissent. There
was only one right way to express political opinion: the
government's way. This resulted in sharply restricted
political activity and little freedom of expression. It
also resulted in a lot of persecution and suffering. The
Communist and Islamic Dawa Parties were forbidden,
Iraqis of Persian origin were exiled, and criticism of any
sort was not tolerated. In short, the government reacted
violently against anyone who dared to speak up.

---

* meaning "new."

3

SCHOOLING

I attended preschool at the Jewish Hesqale Daniel School in Sinnak for one year, and the following year went to kindergarten at the St. Yousif Cathedral School.

I spent my primary school years at the Mar Ephrem Syriac Catholic Coed School in the Alwaiya district of Baghdad. The school was named after St. Ephrem the Syrian (ca. 306-373), a fourth-century Syriac deacon and theologian.

I can't be thankful enough for this wonderful school that was run by nuns. They planted the seeds of Christian faith in me and had a tremendous impact on the rest of my life. Every day we attended morning Mass as soon as we got off the school bus. The church taught me how important it was to repent and confess my sins to a priest. I learned that if we hide even a small sin, we are actually guilty of a greater sin: pride.

We respected the nuns in the school and the monks in the church for their dedication, knowing that they made vows of poverty and consecrated their entire lives in service to Christ and the Church. Generally they lived in convents and monasteries, sharing all things in common, while serving outside in various places. For us children, as well as the church parishioners, the monks and nuns pointed the way to an authentic Christian life. They taught us honesty and truthfulness, for honesty is best learned by following the example of an honest person.

I also used to go regularly with my family to the local Mar Elia Al-Hiry Church in the Baghdad Al-Jadeeda district. This church was named after Mar Elia, an Assyrian monk* from the southern city of Al-Hirah. We attended masses and prayers on Sundays and holidays. The priest often preached on repentance for the forgiveness of sins.

Our church youth group, Akhawiya, organized lectures on different topics and conducted reading and discussion groups on biblical themes. We went on trips together, assisted during church services, and visited the sick. These activities served to deepen our commitment. Our youth group activities certainly strengthened and encouraged me in my inner longing and urge to do what was right. Our church took a strong stand in the area of sexual purity. We did not go on dates, nor did we have any boy-girl relationships, but were as brothers and sisters. This helped me to resist many temptations during my teenage years.

* Mar Elia founded the Dair Mar Elia monastery in the sixth century, just south of Mosul.

But despite my attempts to stand firm against the influences of the culture around me, I still struggled with myself. It was obvious that people, good people— even the best people around me—did not always have high moral standards. My relatives called themselves Christians, but their Christianity ended as they exited the doors of the church each Sunday.

The contradictions weighed on me, making me frustrated, and even desperate. I couldn't seem to find a way out or to find answers to this dilemma. At one point, when I was around fifteen years old, I was so low I had suicidal thoughts. But by the time I was a senior in high school I had managed to gain enough inner strength to surmount evil impulses and stand firm against these temptations.

I began to do well in school and, in fact, got excellent grades, getting high enough scores on my final exams to get into University. So, in the fall of 1976, I entered the Chemical Engineering Department in the Engineering College of the University of Baghdad.

During my time in university, Baba and Julie began to have marital problems. In anger, she would leave the house, moving to a house she owned in another district. Because of the tension, the whole family was dragged down and it began to affect my studies. I became distressed and depressed.

About that time, when I was eighteen, Baba finally bought me a drum kit. Shant, an Armenian neighbor with whom I grew up, played the guitar so we started practicing hard rock together. Within a short time we were performing at engagements, weddings, and parties. We sometimes went into schools and played on stage for dances and other occasions. Once we even played on television during a school competition program. Although we only played for the fun of it, we did get paid enough to rent amplifiers and speakers.

Music loomed large in our lives and became our passion–especially hard rock. We and our friends found the rock music exciting and attractive, although in retrospect it was just senseless, mechanical noise, reflecting my own inner emptiness. We looked down on the more prosaic styles of music–Assyrian and Arabic line dance music and Western dance music–even though we often had to perform them at parties. The atmosphere at events was sometimes sleazy and did not bring me closer to God.

At the same time, I stopped going to church and drifted away from my church friends and youth group, hanging out with a new set. These were kind and sympathetic young Muslims who cared for one another like brothers. Close comrades, we spent a lot of time together. Evenings, we frequented clubs and pubs or we walked the crowded, shop-lined streets of Baghdad.

We had passionate discussions on every imaginable topic. These were heady times as we sought to make sense of the world around us and find purpose in life. We felt liberated and happy.

Although we all expressed having a faith–their Muslim faith and my Christian faith–none of us made more than a cursory effort to live up to it. Each of us was being gradually sucked into things we knew to be wrong–activities that we didn't dare to talk about with each other. As I drifted along with these friends and away from the standards I had espoused in my early youth, especially what I had learned about right and wrong in church and primary school, I too was drawn more and more into activities that troubled my conscience–profanity, sexual relationships, and so forth.

I was disgusted with myself and wanted to change, but the more I struggled, the more firmly I seemed to be stuck in the mire. I became inwardly flabby and self-centered; my conscience was dying, even though a tiny voice inside me was trying to put me back onto the right track. I ignored it, lulled to sleep by my apathy.

4

IRAQ AT WAR

War broke out between Iraq and Iran on September 22, 1980, while I was in my last year at university. It was a stunning blow to the Iraqi populace, as no one could understand why this conflict had erupted. Although we had heard news off and on about problems at the borders, nobody expected it to escalate into war.

Still today there is a lot of speculation about why the war broke out. There had been conflict for years on the border between the two countries, especially over the sharing of the Shatt al-Arab River, which is formed by the confluence of the Euphrates and the Tigris. Fighting began in 1975 between Iraqi and the Iranian-supported Kurds, ending in the Algiers Agreement, wherein Iraq relinquished half of Shatt al-Arab to Iran, and Iran agreed to cease supporting the Kurdish movement in the north of Iraq.

However, tension continued and was exacerbated when Khomeini came to power in Iran and led the

1979 Islamic Revolution. Khomeini had been living in Iraq, but in 1978, because of Iranian pressure, the Iraqi government asked him to leave. Tension mounted due to sectarianism, but was also aggravated by some of the world powers that were manipulating the political situation behind the scenes.

With the outbreak of war, a dreadful atmosphere prevailed throughout the country. Sirens blared in the cities whenever there was incoming Iranian aircraft. Everyone had to rush about and find somewhere to hide. We watched, unbelieving, as Iraqi and Iranian fighter jets fought in the skies just above us, shooting each other down. Surface-to-air anti-aircraft missiles chased after the aircraft. It wasn't long before "war martyrs" started to return: taxi after taxi flooded the streets, each with a coffin on top, covered with an Iraqi flag.

In 1981, out of the blue, the government issued a directive that any university students who had to repeat studies for any reason would be drafted and allowed to finish their exams during their military service. There was a hue and a cry from the academic institutions. Our dean said, mockingly, "How can a student study on the front lines and take his exams?" I heard later that he was fired from his post.

Since I had to repeat two subjects, I was drafted and had to leave the university.

Of course, no one wanted to join the army, but we didn't have any choice. Military service was inescapable, since the government had only one way of dealing with draft dodgers: execution.

Everyone took for granted that joining the army and defending the homeland was the unquestionable duty of every citizen. After all, hasn't this been the lot of people everywhere throughout history? People avoided digging any deeper than this superficial way of thinking, especially when they had not yet experienced the horror of war nor lived to see its bitter fruits. This is, unfortunately, the way we humans are; our conscience is shaken only when we begin to suffer.

I was sent to a center two hours south of Baghdad in the city of Najaf for basic and infantry training, along with hundreds of new recruits. We were put through intense physical training, firearms use, marksmanship, and arms maintenance in order to be ready to fight on the front.

During this time I had the good fortune to be assigned to the commissary store instead of doing hard physical labor under the blazing sun. At that time cigarettes were in high demand and could command double the price on the black market because they were so hard to procure.

One day we received a delivery of cigarettes at the commissary. The supervisor in charge told me to hide them. He was supposed to distribute the cigarettes impartially to whoever came first, and I knew that if I followed his orders, the enlisted men, who most suffered under the impact of army life, wouldn't get any. The foot soldiers were the guys with whom I lived and worked, and they deserved a little pleasure.

But my supervisor wanted to sell the cigarettes solely to officers in order to butter them up and earn privileges. Then the officers would reciprocate if he wanted something. It was beneath the dignity of an officer to stand in line with common soldiers to make purchases, so the store supervisor used to go directly to the officers to give them priority, especially in the case of scarce items. Everyone knew that the war machine was greased by bribes, favoritism, connections, and behind-the-scenes deals, but I was incensed, nonetheless, that the manager was lining his pockets at the expense of my comrades. I ignored his directions and sold the cigarettes fairly to all who came.

When my supervisor found out that I hadn't hidden the cigarettes, but that they were all gone and none of the officers had gotten any, he went ballistic! "I thought I told you to put that delivery in the back room!" he remonstrated, infuriated by my brazenness.

I stood firm, knowing that I had done the right thing. "I know, but when the time came to sell the cigarettes, I sold them to whoever came first. It's not fair to save them all for the officers."

I could almost see smoke coming out of his ears, he was fuming so, but he couldn't call me to account, because he didn't have a legal leg to stand on. However, through gossip and abuse of his authority, he got me dismissed. I had to go back to work with my buddies under the hot sun. I knew I had done the right thing, but I learned that it will cost something if I follow my conscience.

After six months in the training center, I was transferred to a naval construction unit in the southern city of Basra, in the Khamsa Meel district, where we did manual labor night and day.

Although I had never worked so hard in my life, I gave it my best, because I was learning a lot about construction. Once I had to load a truck along with one of my comrades. We had to load five hundred fifty-pound cinder blocks, which we somehow did in only a half hour.

There was a dental clinic near our base, and I learned that anyone having dental treatment could get a day of rest, and anyone who had an extraction could rest for three days. I was so worn out by the work that, like many of my comrades, I started having my teeth pulled. When the authorities discovered what we were doing, they put a stop to rest days.

5

DETENTION

During working hours one day, Salem, a fellow soldier, and I were strolling around the Khamsa Meel market, when we were suddenly accosted by two "Wasps"—military police who wear a distinctive red beret. They were hated and feared by both civilians and military personnel, because of the cavalier way they treated people. They had the authority to arrest anyone on even the least suspicion of misbehavior, so everyone gave them a wide berth.

"Show me your ID," one of them commanded.

I was carrying an official pass to be out during the day, but Salem did not have one.

I showed them my permission slip, and they let me go, but they immediately marched Salem off to an Efa Russian military truck that was hidden in an alley a couple of blocks further on. I kept walking, heading toward where the Wasps had disappeared around a corner with Salem, but as I passed the alley I could see him waving to me, dangling some keys in the air.

I had a valid pass, so I walked up to the truck where a Wasp was standing guard with a weapon in his hands to make sure the delinquent soldiers didn't escape.

As I approached the truck, Salem leaned out of the back and said, "Yacoub, here, take my car keys and drive my car back to my house." Salem lived in Basra, and his house was not far away.

"No problem," I told him, reaching for the keys.

The Wasp suddenly started pushing me into the back of the truck.

"Hey, what are you doing? I'm not one of them!" I shouted indignantly, trying to extricate myself from his grasp.

"Do you have permission to be out here?" he asked, belligerently.

"Yes, of course!"

"Then show me your permission slip."

I showed it to him. He could see that it was valid, but he seemed to be determined to find something wrong. Looking long and hard at my face, he finally said, "Get into the truck. Your beard is not regulation length."

The unwritten rule was that if you scrape a dinar across your cheek it shouldn't make a sound. I had shaved the day before, so my beard had grown a bit, but I knew it wasn't too long. The Wasp was being picky and had the authority to make up the rules as he went along.

Incensed, I tried to splutter a protest, but words wouldn't come out. He ordered me into the back of the truck, so I obeyed, knowing that it was useless to argue. Just like that, we were being led off to prison like common criminals, but I was powerless to do anything about it.

I learned later that the sergeant of this unit had ordered his men to bring in a "harvest" of fifty heads each day. As soon as they got their quota, they drove away to their unit–prison. I had been in the wrong place at the wrong time.

When we arrived at the prison, we were ordered to stand in a row in front of an upside-down metal container. One by one, we sat for a haircut. Everybody got a close-cropped "number zero" haircut just to humiliate us–a standard punishment. Salem lied to the barber, telling him that he was getting engaged next weekend. The barber had compassion on him and left his hair a bit longer, but he cut gouges here and there to make it look as if he was trying to make my friend look ridiculous. The barber would have been punished if he hadn't done something to humiliate us. "When you get out of here," he whispered in Salem's ear, "you can trim your hair and it will look okay."

They herded us into an old shipping container two and a half meters wide and six meters long. There was hardly enough room to stand as we were fifty men packed into this small area. There were no windows, and the only air we got was from a small hole in the wall where the metal had been torn.

We could hardly breathe. It was summer, and the sun beat down unmercifully on the metal, baking us inside. The only toilet facility inside the container was a can in the corner that smelled so bad no one would go near it. The can overflowed onto the floor, and as the men tried to edge away from the wet area around the can, we were squashed more and more.

At night we had to sleep sitting up, leaning against one another. I was lucky to have the metal wall at my back. Because of the humid conditions in our prison, as well as the high humidity in the Basra region, condensation on the ceiling constantly dripped down on us all night.

The next day at around nine in the morning we were lined up in three rows outside the container. Several names were called out, and these men were sent back to their units. This military unit was expected to do construction work, but each day they recruited several prisoners to do their strenuous work as a punishment.

We followed the same routine every day: after roll call a number of the prisoners would be sent back to their units. Others would either be sent back into the container or assigned to the workforce, where they did hard physical labor. I felt so trapped and entombed inside the container that I quickly learned to volunteer for work at each opportunity, just to be able to stay outside.

On the second day, I listened for my name. They called Salem's name but not mine. By the third day I suspected that my name was not on their list at all, so I rushed over to the soldier with the list.

"Hey, where are you going," two of the guards shouted, running after me with their weapons in their hands.

I got to the soldier with the list before they caught me.

"It's okay," I called back to them. "I've been here for three days and my name has not been called. I'm just checking to make sure my name is on the list."

They stood next to me, ready to haul me back to the container when I was done.

The guard with the list asked me for my name.

"Yacoub Yousif," I replied.

He ran his finger up and down the list, but my name wasn't there. Ah, so that's why they were keeping me so long.

"Can you please add me to the list," I pleaded. I was so distraught! Would they have kept me here for a year if I had not asked?

The fourth day they finally called my name.

Since my unit belonged to the navy, I was sent to the main naval prison in Basra and had to stay there for another day. I was sinking into a depression and felt like I was shriveling up inside. How long would I have to endure this treatment—and all because of a shave!

At this naval prison I saw prisoners serving terms of up to ten years. Each prison has a "boss," a prisoner who dominates over the other prisoners, controlling them with violence and cruelty. The boss in this prison had a long Fu Manchu mustache. I avoided him and gave him all due respect.

Finally, on the fifth day after my arrest a guard came to my cell.

"I'm going to take you back to your unit," he said, as he called me from the cell. To my consternation, he started to put handcuffs on me.

This was the last straw. I started screaming and shouting, "No! No! I refuse to put up with this! I never did anything wrong! I'm innocent! Why are you treating me like a criminal?" The stress and humiliation of this unjust treatment was breaking my spirit.

The guard was understanding and tried to calm me down. He whispered in my ear, "Don't worry, this is just standard procedure. I'll take the handcuffs off as soon as we get in the car outside."

He took me to the car and drove me to the main Naval Construction Directorate that was responsible for my unit. There, he handed me over to a lieutenant. I felt out of place in this spotlessly clean, air-conditioned office, I with five-day's growth on my chin and dirty, disheveled clothes.

I knew this lieutenant. He had been one of my colleagues in the College of Engineering. When he saw me, he shook his head, upset at the way I had been treated. He could see that my beard was longer than my hair, since I had not been able to shave for so many days.

"Go on back to your unit," he said, softly.

I tried to stop at the barbershop on the way to get a haircut, but the barber was shocked by my appearance. To get rid of me, he said, "No, no, we don't do beards!"

If he was shocked, I was devastated—not so much by his rejection, but by the hell I had just been through. How could one person treat another as I had been treated over the past five days? I had been herded like an animal, worked like a slave, chained like a savage, and intimidated as though I was less than human. Was there any place on earth that practiced justice, equality, and respect for human rights?

6

TO THE BATTLEFIELD

During that time, I was sent out on construction projects to the town of Al-Faw, a beautiful town located on the Shatt al-Arab River, with Iran on the far bank. Some families had relatives on both sides of the river. This town was on the front and had Iranian and Iraqi forces facing off on either side of the river. The whole town, along with its extensive date-palm orchards, was laid waste.

Because people had to flee abruptly due to the sudden outbreak of hostilities, they were not able to take anything with them. Many families put an open Qur'an on their beds in an attempt to appeal to the conscience of the Iraqi soldiers who fought their way into town. Unfortunately, in a destructive frenzy, both officers and enlisted men brazenly looted the property of the Al-Faw residents. They went so far as to uproot and ship home the palm trees of the district that bore such excellent fruit.

Of course, not all soldiers had such wanton disregard for other people's belongings. Many of the Iraqi soldiers acted with good conscience, but this attack gave me a lot to think about.

After about a year and a half in the construction unit, hundreds of us were transferred into an intensive fighting school for a couple of months, to prepare us for transfer to fighting units at the front.

One day we were divided into groups to be sent to the various fighting brigades at the front. None of us wanted to go as we knew that it meant going into battle, but we had to follow orders. A sergeant read off the letters of the Arabic alphabet, and we were supposed to separate into groups according to the first letter of our first name.

When he was done there was still one soldier standing there.

The sergeant asked him, "What are you doing there?"

"Well, sir," he replied, "the first letter of my name wasn't called out."

"What do you mean, the first letter of your name wasn't called out? I went through the whole alphabet!"

"Well sorry, I never heard it."

Looking down at his list, the sergeant said, "What's the first letter of your name?"

"*Edh.*"

Casting a withering look at the soldier, the sergeant said, "There's no such letter in Arabic! What's your name?"

"Dhapher," the soldier answered.

The sergeant rolled his eyes and moaned. "Look, Dhapher, your name starts with the letter *dh* not *edh*. Didn't you learn anything in school?"

"No, sir, I never went to school. I'm illiterate."

Shaking his head, the officer said, "Go on, join the *dh* group over there."

We were all chuckling, because we knew that Dhapher was putting it on to avoid having to go.

He joined the same group as mine. Since he owned his own bus, he kindly offered to transport us all to the Fourty-Fourth Infantry Brigade at the front in the Amarah region. When we arrived in the region, Dhapher left his bus behind the lines, and we continued on by military transport to brigade headquarters, which was on the front lines.

There we were divided into three groups, each destined for a different regiment. We were standing in our groups at the foot of a hill, the other side of which was bare desert. As we stood there, a sergeant lectured us about the fighting at the front. We were raw recruits and had no conception of what the front was, so we were relaxed, making jokes and snickering behind the sergeant's back.

At that moment we heard a soft boom. We paid no attention to it and continued to horse around, but seconds later we jumped when we heard a strong swooshing noise, followed by an explosion about a hundred meters away. Then we heard whizzing noises and saw curious little objects sticking in the soil on the hillside next to us. We were clueless as to what was happening and started questioning each other.

"What was that?"

"No idea."

"Do you think that was a bomb!"

"A bomb? No way!"

"It could have been..."

"A bomb?"

"Yes, it *is* a bomb," the sergeant confirmed, shaking his head. "That's shrapnel in the hill over there. And by the way," he added with a smirk, "the next time you hear incoming, I recommend you hit the dirt if you don't want to get riddled with holes like that hill."

Our smiles vanished as we began to grasp the awful reality of our situation.

Forty of us were billeted in a bunker for the night, and next morning we headed off to our respective regiments. Since we didn't have any duties yet, most of us returned to the bunker. That evening there was a lot of heavy bombing.

One of our comrades came rushing into our barracks, moaning, "He's dead."

"What? Who's dead? What are you blabbering about?"

The rest of us rushed over to hear the news.

"Mahmoud was killed," the comrade said, breathlessly.

"You mean Mahmoud, who came with us today?"

"Yes, that's him. He went out to buy something from the commissary store and was hit by a lot of shrapnel."

We swallowed hard. Staring at the floor, we tried to comprehend what was happening. We had only just arrived, and already one of our number was dead. What was in store for the rest of us? Each one asked himself, "Will I survive?" I wondered, anxiously, if *any* of us would survive. This was war in all its glory.

7

WAKING TO REALITY

It took army life to awaken me to the bitter truths of life in my country: blatant inequality, injustices of every kind, institutionalized slavery, and restricted freedom—especially freedom of expression. Our society in general seemed to be structured on hypocrisy and falsehood, but this was especially evident in the army. The gears of the army were greased with bribes, favoritism, connections, and behind-the-scenes manipulation.

During the war, the government gave substantial material inducements to the professional military staff—high salaries and bigger mortgage loans, as well as other perks. For instance, the government ordinarily gave out a 1,000-dinar "marriage grant" for couples getting married, but military personnel got three times that amount. Professional staff could purchase a new car for one dinar. Depending on their rank, they could get a Brazilian-made Volkswagen Passat, a Mitsubishi, a Toyota Crown Super Saloon, or a Mercedes.

The unfortunate thing about the distribution of free cars to military staff was that most of them had never learned to drive. Consequently, they bribed officials to get a driver's license, and this led to an increase in traffic accidents. An article in the newspaper Al-Thawra* reported that in 1985 alone there were around sixty thousand traffic accidents resulting in serious injuries and deaths.

One of the most disgusting aspects of the graft and dishonesty was the way those with means could buy their way out. Old and disabled people ended up at the front, while well-to-do people with political connections stayed in the rear lines or back in the cities, even though they were perfectly healthy. I once saw a soldier whose sight was so bad that he needed somebody to lead him about, but he was still at the front.

The coffins of dead soldiers began to flood the cities and villages. The war, like some bizarre harvest combine, was reaping thousands of souls on both sides, many of them civilians. Many who were not killed lost limbs or had other serious injuries. There were thousands of widows and orphans. Many people became refugees or were forced to emigrate, because they lost houses, jobs, businesses, or farms. Worse still, people were losing their ethical principles. A deep depression swept over the country.

The war front extended along the whole border between Iraq and Iran. No one can truly feel the horror

---

* meaning "The Revolution."

of war until they have been to the front line of a battle—the deafening noise, eruptions on every side from falling artillery shells, screams, blood flowing in rivulets from the mangled bodies of soldiers who only moments before were our comrades.

Our battlefield barracks were designed to be quickly constructed and dismantled. The walls were made of sandbags, and the roofs were wooden slats covered with sheets of corrugated steel with a layer of dirt on top. They provided little protection from the shelling and bombing.

We were always under fire from artillery and mortar shells, penetration bombs, and air blast bombs—bombs which explode in the air before hitting the ground. There was the constant barrage of Iranian bullets buzzing around us, shells that were shot wildly—especially in the evening as we were walking about our unit. After a while, we barely paid attention to them, we were so used to hearing gunfire. In any case there wasn't anything we could do about it; we didn't have any way to protect ourselves. If we were hit, we were dead; if not, we were alive. There was so much death around us that life became a game of roulette.

I myself came under heavy fire a number of times. On one occasion I was riding in the back of a military truck together with three other soldiers. A 120-millimeter mortar shell fell about four meters behind us, and I was sure it was all over for me. The truck veered sharply right and then left, knocked off course by the powerful explosion but, miraculously, none of us were hurt—not even the truck.

Once a soldier in our company tread on a land mine while on night patrol in no man's land. Nothing was left of his foot but a mass of bloody tendrils. The medic didn't know what to do, so he cut the tendrils away with scissors.

In another incident, as our platoon was crossing a small bridge leading toward the enemy, a 60-millimeter mortar shell landed between the legs of our platoon leader. Amazingly, he was not killed, but the shrapnel sliced off both his feet. He was immediately rushed behind the front to the hospital. As he was being transported from the bridge, one of the soldiers had the presence of mind to take the severed feet as well. Luckily, military doctors were able to sew his feet on again. After he healed, the officer was able to walk again.

Another soldier was hit in the back by shrapnel. His twin brother, who was with him in the same platoon, panicked. Unable to think clearly because of the shock, he picked up his brother and carried him into an orchard in the direction of the enemy. Exhausted from running, he laid his brother on the ground and told him to stay put, while he ran to find someone who could help get him to a hospital.

As he raced back behind the lines, he fell unconscious from shock and exhaustion and had to be taken to the hospital. Two days later he awoke from a coma and, remembering his brother, cried out in agony, "My brother!"

He ran back with some comrades to the orchard to find his brother, but all he found was some tracks on the ground. Following them, he found the body of his dead brother some distance away.

I met a soldier who claimed to have had a "sex change" after a bit of shrapnel penetrated the back of his head. He showed me pictures, and it was true that he had been a strapping big bodybuilder before he was hurt. But when I met him he had the slender figure of a woman with breasts. His fiancée broke off their engagement. In spite of this, he didn't apply for a discharge, since no one would have dreamed of doing that during wartime. He only asked to be moved back behind the front line.

Once, Hunnah, one of my relatives, was trying to flee with a fellow soldier from a dangerous situation during a feverish battle. As he was running, he looked over at his friend, who was running without a head. Even though a whirring piece of shrapnel had beheaded the poor man, his body kept running for some distance before collapsing. My relative was so shocked that he blacked out and had to be hospitalized for a month. He was unable to talk because of the psychological trauma.

Since we were fighting in the desert, snakes and scorpions, both yellow and black, were our constant companions. At night when we were trying to sleep, rats would slink furtively into our barracks in the dark and nibble our fingers and toes. They also constantly attacked the latrines that we built, destroying them.

In the corner of the bunker where I slept, there was a hole near where I placed my head at night. One afternoon, while I was sitting talking with my comrades, I happened to look up and see a snake emerge from the hole and look around the inside of the bunker. After taking in the scene, the snake must have been bored, because it turned around and left. There was so much danger lurking about day and night that I didn't even give the snake a thought and continued to sleep in the same place.

Once when I was sitting cross-legged on my bed, a mother scorpion trotted along the edge of the bed followed by several baby scorpions. I grabbed one of my flip-flops and squashed them one by one.

Another time a group of soldiers squatted in a circle around a huge black scorpion that was trapped under a jar on the ground. They dug a little trench around the jar with a stick, and poured fuel oil into the trench. After lighting the oil with a match, they removed the jar to see what the scorpion would do. It tried to move first in one direction, then another. But of course it was surrounded by flames. Not being able to escape, it appeared to sting itself in the neck and died.

As dangerous and annoying as these creatures were, they were like friends in comparison to the misery of the battlefield. The specter of death seemed to roam triumphantly wherever I turned. I had entered a terrifying world—a realm on the border of hell. Everyone was frightened. Faces were pale with fear, terror, and exhaustion. Even the hardiest men were often reduced to cowering, whimpering children.

The enemy was a mere seventy-five meters away from us. Bombs, bullets, and shrapnel were continually flying in every direction. The dead and dying were on every side. And I was tormented—not only by the horror of war, but also by a burden of guilt.

With death staring me in the face day after day, I cried out in agony, "Enough!" I knew I was not right with God, following a sinful course, and needing to turn my life around. I humbled myself and asked God to forgive me.

8

FROM DEATH TO LIFE

That was the most decisive moment of my life. It felt like a veil had been lifted from my eyes and I could see the clear light of God for the first time since I had turned away from him in my youth. I had been shackled by sin. Now I felt the chains of evil falling away from me. I was truly free. What I had thought for years was freedom had actually been enslavement to dark powers.

On my first furlough after experiencing repentance, I went back to my church for the first time in seven years. I knelt inside the confessional and poured my heart out to our priest, Philip Helayi, without hiding anything. I felt the seriousness of the time and could not waste another minute. I felt like this was the beginning of a new life for me.

After going to confession and attending a worship service, I felt as light as a feather. A heavy burden had been lifted from my heart and conscience. I experienced the free forgiveness from the living Christ that was made possible through the blood He shed on the cross.

Despite the horror at the front and the depression that was crushing the whole country, an overwhelming joy washed over me like ocean waves breaking on the sand. I still had to face many risks, but I now felt an inner security. I had experienced the power of the Holy Spirit and the grace of salvation that guarantees eternal life. From now on I wanted to take an uncompromising stand for Jesus Christ and his commandments, especially his Sermon on the Mount.

Whenever I passed a church in Baghdad, my conscience accused me because I hadn't noticed it when I used to roam the streets with my friends. "Where were all these churches? Why hadn't I noticed them before?" I wondered. So I started visiting them, weeping bitterly about my past and how I had lived. How on earth had I missed the pure heavenly air of those churches? How had I missed this wholesome, chaste atmosphere?

I began to spend a lot of time at church events. I took lay courses in theology in *Al-Centre,* the Christian Cultural Centre in Baghdad, and attended a small-group Bible study under the direction of Father Lucien Cup, a Belgian monk who had been serving the churches in Iraq for over fifty years. Throughout my furlough I attended morning mass at St. George Church and evening mass with the nuns at St. Joseph Cathedral Church.

Knowing how I was influenced by the atmosphere

in the dance halls and music venues, I stopped playing music altogether.

At the end of my furlough I had to return to my unit. Back at the front, I missed the church atmosphere and my Christian friends, but I gained strength by reading my pocket New Testament, as well as by listening to the daily Arabic-language Christian broadcasts from Trans World Radio. Nana used to listen to TWR every day at bedtime, and she was the one who had told me about this station.

I couldn't live or move at the front without prayer, because I knew that my salvation was in the hands of Jesus. I had an open, personal relationship with him—direct access to the Lord of the universe. I needed him terribly throughout the horrible and bloody period of the war.

Of course, many people have found this relationship with Christ. Once, while on furlough, I got to know three devoted old sisters—Irene, Daisy, and Gladys—who never ceased to pray, frequently attending prayers and masses in different churches. I loved to visit them as they comforted me and encouraged me to "rejoice always." Knowing that I was in constant danger, they exhorted me to not worry because, as they said, "Jesus is with you, even at the front."

They suggested that I pray the Twenty-Third Psalm whenever I found myself at the front. These words have been a comfort to millions of people throughout the ages:

The Lord *is* my shepherd;
I shall not want.
He makes me to lie down in green pastures;
He leads me beside the still waters.
He restores my soul;
He leads me in the paths of righteousness
For His name's sake.
Yea, though I walk through the valley of the shadow of
    death,
I will fear no evil;
For you *are* with me;
Your rod and Your staff, they comfort me.
You prepare a table before me in the presence of my
    enemies;
You anoint my head with oil;
My cup runs over.
Surely goodness and mercy shall follow me
All the days of my life;
And I will dwell in the house of the LORD forever. (NKJV)

Reciting the Twenty-Third Psalm was such a help that I continued to do it long after leaving the army. I also prayed the Lord's Prayer, as well as praying the rosary, but I gradually replaced the fifty "Hail Marys" with fifty recitations of the Lord's Prayer alone, since I was desperate for Jesus.

As I read my Bible and prayed, I was drawn into a closer and closer relationship with God. I came into contact with all sorts of characters in the army, but I learned that God loves all people, regardless of their background, even though he hates their evil deeds. He has patience with each one, so that they might have a chance to turn away from sin. Jesus said that there will be more rejoicing in heaven over one person who turns from sin than over ninety-nine persons who do not need to repent. So I also had to love all people, but hate sin.

I had experienced the joy of forgiveness, a gift from God, which gave me inner security and true peace. Reading the words of Jesus and the apostles, I learned that this peace had to flow out from me to make way for loving and harmonious relationships. I could be an instrument to help break down interpersonal barriers. God's peace was not meant to be only a cessation of hostility, but an attitude that he places in the heart of a person. Jesus said that the peace he gives is different from the peace the world offers. It is an inner peace that helps us live above the challenges of daily life. I wanted that peace—for me as well as for those around me.

I prayed that our whole country might find new life. I knew that if both the people and the leaders of a nation would humble themselves before God and seek repentance and forgiveness, they would be compelled by love to share their resources with the peoples around them. Then nations would be able to stand together and assist one another, eliminating poverty and need. Peace would prevail and wars would end. Maybe this was "pie in the sky," but I believed that God could really change hearts.

After I repented, Jesus overwhelmed me with his love and filled a void in my heart. I was more confident and outgoing. He wiped away the anxiety and insecurity I had felt ever since the divorce of my parents and the difficult years of my childhood. He opened my eyes to things in my life that still needed to change, and he filled my heart with joy. So love began to flow out from my heart, often leading to service to others.

I started seeing the image of God in the faces of those around me. As I did so I became more and more aware of the needs of those who were poor and needy and distressed, and looked for ways to reach out to them. My heart was filled with a great love for all people, regardless of their religion or race—including our Iranian enemies, of course. Why? Because Jesus sacrificed himself on the cross to save all people everywhere, whether they be Middle Eastern, North or South American, European, Asian, or African.

I found a warm relationship with all my fellow soldiers, regardless of their faith or background. We often got together and offered advice to each other. I tried to encourage all—whether Christian or Muslim—to turn away from wrong and to turn to God in prayer. One day, a fellow Christian soldier who had just returned from furlough, came joyfully to me and told me that Jesus had given him the strength to break with a long-term sexual relationship.

A Muslim soldier I knew went through a traumatic experience after running away from the army. When he was caught, he was sent to prison. One day many busses full of prisoners arrived, and the inmates were herded into a large hall. Ten by ten, the prisoners were tied to wooden columns along a wall, blindfolded, and shot to death.

My friend stood by, agonizing, as he waited his turn. Finally, he was taken and blindfolded. As the executioners were aiming their rifles, a voice barked, "Ready, aim..."

"Stop! Stop!"

A messenger rushed in breathlessly, and everyone turned to see what he was shouting about.

"The president has pardoned all these prisoners," the messenger exclaimed in a loud voice.

My friend was saved. He promised God that he would change the way he lived and become a good Muslim. Repenting of his previous lifestyle, he began to pray and to do what he considered to be right according to Islam. When he was allowed to return to his unit we became best of friends–like brothers. I tried to encourage him to continue to live for God.

On another occasion, one of my supervisors from the southern city of Nasiriyah asked me if he could borrow my Bible, despite warnings from his religious leaders. Some of the soldiers joked with him saying, "What's up? Are you going to become a Christian?"

But he answered, "No, I'm just going to read it for five minutes to get an idea of what it's all about. I've never read it before."

We were in a bunker at the front in the heat of the blazing desert. He sat on the cool dirt floor and began to read. Five minutes passed...ten minutes...twenty minutes...a half hour. He was still engrossed in his reading. The Gospel narrative gripped him so much that he couldn't put the book down. After one and a half hours he stood up, surprised and amazed at the spirit of the Gospels.

He handed the Bible back to me, and said, "Wow, what a book!" Then he went away very quietly, mulling over what he had read.

There are some aspects of military life that are beneficial. For instance, the physical exercise and personal discipline can have a positive impact. Each morning we had to shave, polish our shoes, tidy our clothes, have breakfast, wash dishes, and make our beds—all before six o'clock roll call. Morning calisthenics followed. During the day we did construction and maintenance work, most of which was quite physical. This toughened the body, and helped combat indolence and slackness. We learned to be grateful for what we had, because our meals and food were simple.

There are also certain social and cultural rewards to being in the military, since we worked shoulder-to-shoulder with people from a variety of cultures and traditions. Just being constantly together engenders camaraderie among people with diverse cultural and ethnic backgrounds. Many people had never before met a Christian and, consequently, had negative views of Christianity. But through living closely together, they grew to love us, realizing that Christians are also human beings.

Nevertheless, I wished I was able to find the kind of deep fellowship in civil society back home that I found among my army comrades. On furlough, I certainly got inner strength from worshipping and praying in church, but when the mass was over, everyone dispersed to his or her home and didn't seek out fellowship until the next service. This disappointed me, as I was hungering for Christian fellowship.

I became more and more convinced that Christ is not interested in Sunday Christians. He wants his people to work and worship together all day, every day, giving themselves in service to each other and to the world around them.

9

WHY WAR?

Now that I had reset the compass of my life, I began to think more deeply about the question of war and what causes it. First of all, I had to admit that I had been the cause of war, because war is only a reflection of the human condition. When we stop listening to the voice of conscience, when we open ourselves up to evil thoughts and actions, when we close our hearts to our fellow humans, then war is inevitable—whether it be the petty "war" of family infighting, or the major conflagrations that tear the world apart.

And what purpose was war serving, when it is quite obvious that the result has been millions of victims—both soldiers and civilians?

We know that so-called smart bombs are not really so smart. Thousands of civilians lose their lives senselessly in bombing raids that are purportedly aimed at military targets. We have a wonderful euphemism for these tragic deaths: collateral damage. But as one military expert suggested, maybe these are not actually "accidents." Maybe they are calculated to incite people to overthrow their government. Civilians are convenient pawns in the drive for political power.

During war people are forced to leave their homes, their towns, their land, their businesses, their farms, creating enormous refugee problems. Many no longer have access to food, shelter, schools, or medical care and often end up homeless or in refugee camps, which leads to social unrest and a self-perpetuating cycle of illiteracy and poverty. This is also often the breeding ground of militias, rebels, and terrorists.

In Iraq, civilians resented the increased immigration of foreign workers to replace the thousands of Iraqis who were being conscripted into the army. Although these workers were paid low wages, they enjoyed a stable civilian life and were thankful to be able to send money to their poor families in their home countries while Iraqi men were fighting on the battlefield. At the time of the war against Iran, there were five million Egyptians in Iraq, as well as many Sudanese. This also led to lower wages, higher unemployment, and housing shortages among those Iraqis who were still at home. Naturally, this caused resentment against the foreigners, even though they were mostly Arabs and Muslims, and they suffered much abuse.

War is human greed writ large: ambition, avarice, the drive to dominate, pride, and hate. The Bible tells us:

> What causes fights and quarrels among you? Don't they come from your desires that battle within you? You desire but do not have, so you kill. You covet but you cannot get what you want, so you quarrel and fight. You do not have because you do not ask God. When you ask, you do not receive, because you ask with wrong motives, that you may spend what you get on your pleasures (James 4:1-3).

Then there are the demonic tools of warfare. Bomb casings are made out of an alloy that is especially designed to disintegrate into fragments with sharp, razor-like edges. When these bombs and shells reach their targets they explode into shrapnel–thousands of little spiraling missiles that fly at incredibly high speeds, lacerating bodies and destroying property. Shells are sometimes made from depleted uranium, which is radioactive and causes cancer and birth defects.

There are, of course, bullets. Millions of rounds of them, and bayonets used in hand-to-hand combat. Chemical gases and biological weapons, although forbidden by international law, are nonetheless widely used.

And then there are reprehensible practices aimed at keeping warfare on the move. In Iraq, execution squads were stationed at intersections to execute deserters–immediately and without a trial–in order to "discourage" soldiers from leaving their fighting units during offensives.

But who is benefiting? Not the common people! High government and military figures earn fortunes through graft and deception. Arms manufacturers rake in hundreds of millions through the sale of their products. Politicians exploit the war machine for their own personal advantage and set their sights on higher offices with the illusory platform of "freedom and democracy."

Generally speaking, neither the Iraqi nor the Iranian populace wanted war, but citizens were forced to join their respective armies because it was compulsory. There is a story that once during a military offensive, an Iraqi and an Iranian met by chance in a bunker, having escaped the hellish bombing. They agreed not to kill one another, but to wait for the end of the fighting. The soldier of the winning army would take the other soldier prisoner, thus insuring that they both survived—with their conscience intact!

Thousands of Iraqi soldiers fled from the front and went into hiding. Some lived in secret, using false furlough vouchers or false identity cards. Others escaped to other countries. In fact, thousands emigrated from both Iraq and Iran to avoid getting killed in the conflict. This was the only safe way they could protest against the government and its bloody warmongering spirit.

Those who had money—and there were many—did not have to resort to leaving the country; they could pay off officials, who would pull their relatives to safety behind the front lines. This, of course, lined the pockets of the military leaders. Baba would probably have resorted to this stratagem on my behalf had he known some high official to whom he could turn for help.

The government launched huge propaganda campaigns to brainwash young people into signing up. These hyped-up, patriotic broadcasts were aimed at recruiting the largest possible number of young people. Although military service in Iraq was mandatory, the government also used material incentives to attract young people to volunteer. These young people were tempted by offers of high salaries, priority in food lines in the marketplace, cars that could be purchased for one dinar, and higher-value mortgage loans.

Once a fellow soldier lamented: "I requested permission to buy a plot of land from my local government five years ago but never received a reply. But now they try to induce me to enlist by making all kinds of promises on the defense posters that are splashed all over the city. Do they really think I will believe them?"

During the war the government also lured many young people into the army by promising them assignments to non-fighting branches, like sports teams, music ensembles, or choirs. Once enlisted, these new soldiers soon found themselves at the front to fulfill the "greater need of the Fatherland"—a bitter deception.

I had a bunker mate who volunteered as a wrestler, but a year or so later he was sent to the front, ending up in my regiment. Depressed from being cheated in such an egregious way, he started taking three or four sleeping pills at a time, which drugged him for up to three days straight. Upon waking he would take another batch. At times he overstayed furloughs by as many as five days, despite the fact that being AWOL that long consti- tuted desertion. Fortunately, we had an understanding commander who overlooked his erratic behavior.

As we have seen so many times throughout history– and this is especially true in the Arab world today– *violence begets violence.* Turning young Iraqis into killing machines only served to intensify hate and intolerance, leading to more violence and revenge, and provoking social disintegration.

The government supposedly sent the soldiers into battle to fight for the "cause," but in truth they had no choice. Suddenly they found themselves in the middle of heated, bloody battles and were forced to kill or be killed. Each time they were forced to snuff out the life of another human being, they also destroyed a part of their own souls, leading to anxiety, depression, and guilt. To cope they had to develop a hard exterior in order to not be vulnerable. Day by day, their rage and hatred against the enemy increased–something the govern- ment purposely wanted to instill in them to gain their support. They were completely unaware that the true enemy was the régime that put them into this situation in the first place.

Once the commander of one of my units gave an impassioned speech, telling us, "You should be willing to die as martyrs for the sake of our country." This gave me pause for reflection. I had to ask myself: What do I

really want to die for—what do I want to fight and sacri-
fice my life for? Do I really want to give my life in war,
which causes so much destruction and suffering, and
the only purpose of which is to make some men richer
and more powerful?

Each time I returned to my battalion after a furlough,
my superiors would thrust my RPK* into my hands and
send me straight to the front. This put me in a quandary.
If I were to believe the words of Jesus and the message
of the gospel, now that I was committed to following
Christ, I no longer had the right to kill for any reason.

The great and merciful God of the universe created
humankind—the most precious jewel of all he created.
What makes us imagine that we can defy God and
justify the killing of this perfect creature that he placed
at the pinnacle of creation?

And yet we see the wanton destruction of our fellow
creatures from one end of the world to the other. How
often these horrors are perpetuated in the name of God
or Allah or, worse, in the name of Jesus, the Prince of
Peace!

If you kill someone, no matter how evil he may be,
you are stealing his chance to repent and change his life.
The evil person does not know that he is evil until the
light of God enters his heart. Our task is to forgive, just
as Jesus prayed for his murderers on the cross, saying,

---

* *Ruchnoy Pulemjot Kalashnikova*, meaning "Kalashnikov handheld (light)
machine gun."

"Father, forgive them, for they do not know what they are doing" (Luke 23:34).

I agonized over this question. On Sundays I heard the message of love to Christ and love to my neighbor. In the Bible, the Old Testament commanded, "Thou shalt not kill" (Exod. 20:13), and the New Testament said, "Love your enemies; do good to them that hate you" (Matt. 5:44). But whenever I was on furlough and went to church, there were no sermons against war. On the contrary, on television we saw church patrons paying allegiance to the president.

One of my friends who had studied theology told me, "Don't be stupid! Don't let the enemy kill you! We Christians have to prove that we are just as good citizens as anyone else by defending our homeland!"

I just couldn't buy this. In a way it seemed right and convincing, and many deeply religious people do believe it, but it didn't jive with the commands of Jesus in the Gospels. It wasn't up to me to judge either those in the church or those who agreed with war. I needed to love them and hope that they would repent and receive the same forgiveness I had received.

Anyone who has experienced repentance will understand what I'm saying, but those who haven't experienced it, and whose lives haven't been transformed yet, will not understand how a person can be changed from the inside out by the light of Jesus. They won't comprehend the meaning of forgiveness, but will continue to try to fight evil with evil.

So, I spent hours in prayer, and finally came to the clear conviction that I had to follow the commandment of Christ not to spill blood, whatever consequences I might have to endure. But this wasn't so easy in practice.

10

I CAN DIE BUT I CANNOT KILL

Jesus was absolutely clear when he said: "You have heard that it was said, 'Eye for eye, and tooth for tooth.' But I tell you, do not resist an evil person" (Matt. 5:38).

In fact, Jesus strikes at the heart of the matter when he adds:

> You have heard that it was said to the men of old, "You shall not kill; and whoever kills shall be liable to judgment." But I say to you that everyone who is angry with his brother shall be liable to judgment; whoever insults his brother shall be liable to the council, and whoever says, "You fool!" shall be liable to the hell of fire. (Matt. 5:21-22, RSV)

Pretty serious words; I not only shouldn't kill, I wasn't even supposed to get angry and call someone an idiot! Christ commanded us to love one another as brothers and sisters, and to live in peace and love. On a national or international scale this means that we mustn't go around violating each other's rights, occupying each other's lands, or egging each other on to violence.

Jesus himself had to put this into practice when he was surrounded by soldiers in the Garden of Gethsemane. Peter drew a sword and cut off the ear of the high priest's servant. Laying his hand on the servant and healing him, Jesus commanded Peter: "Put your sword back in its place, for all who draw the sword will die by the sword" (Matt. 26:52).

So, I was now faced with the serious challenge: *Shouldn't I, then, put my sword away?*

At first I thought I would simply go to the military authorities and tell them that I could no longer participate in the army because my faith forbids me to harm other people. But I was afraid; I knew that they would certainly execute me on the spot as a lawbreaker and traitor. Moreover, I didn't have a strong case, as no church that I knew of would support me.

Then I considered another plan: I would defect to the Iranian side and seek asylum there. However, it was highly probable that the Iranians would torture me to try to extract strategic military information. And if I defected, my family would surely be interrogated and harassed by the Iraqi government.

Many university graduates volunteered to become professional army officers. They were immediately promoted to the rank of second lieutenant, buying into the hazy world of perks and privileges. Since I was a chemical engineer, I was tempted to go this route. In this way, I would be relatively safe behind the front lines and receive both civil and military honor as well.

Another way to avoid going to the front was to apply for a military-related job in the civil sector. Those producing arms and weapons could avoid the battlefield. But that also did not set well with my conscience. After all, I would be contributing to the violence just as much as if I were fighting.

A third route that was tempting was to apply to work in the Iraqi intelligence service—a job away from the military. This work was most certainly alien to the way of Jesus and was just another trap. All these tempting paths were nothing but compromises with the devil. Jesus warned us: "For what will it profit them if they gain the whole world but forfeit their life?" (Matt. 16:26). No, I knew that none of these ways were open to me.

So I had no choice but to stay in the army, hoping that the war would soon come to an end. I vowed to myself, however, that if I came face to face with an enemy, I wouldn't kill him, but rather let him kill me. This was not an easy decision to make; it demanded lots of tears and intense prayers for God's strength.

Some people might misunderstand me and call me a coward or traitor. But I was trapped between Christ and

Caesar. The government was commanding me to bear arms and kill people, while Christ was commanding me to die for my faith rather than compromise divine principles.

It takes courage to live by your conscience and swim upstream. As the saying goes, only dead fish go with the flow. How easy it is to kill and destroy, but how much effort it takes to build up, striving for peace and love! I was willing to die for Christ, but I was not willing to kill for anyone, regardless of the consequences. I knew I could suffer hardships—even execution—for this stand.

Yet, God is faithful, meeting us right where we are. Three months after I made my decision never to kill, He opened an incredible door for me.

II

A WAY OUT

Around seven or eight o'clock one evening the whole Third Regiment was roused: Colonel Qais, commander of the Forty-Fourth Brigade, wanted to see Yacoub! Where is Yacoub?

When the messengers finally found me they led me straight to brigade headquarters to meet with him. As I walked away from my billet in hell, I thought I had died and gone to heaven. I never dreamed I would be invited for a personal interview with a colonel. All the way to headquarters I asked myself why he would want to see me—an ordinary foot soldier.

Entering command headquarters I was blown away. Coming in from the dirt and grime of the field, I entered a super-deluxe, multi-room bunker, with a carpeted floor, walls paneled with expensive wood, and a large-screen TV in the corner. The bunker was furnished with a luxurious desk, exquisite overstuffed sofas, bright lights, and, wonder of wonders, air conditioning—all this just behind the front!

I stood stock still at attention and saluted the colonel.

He started asking me questions about myself, my background, and my training. He told me he intended to build a new house in Baghdad, and wondered if I were able to assist him in its construction, thinking that I was a civil engineer.

"Sorry, sir," I answered. I am not a civil engineer; I'm a chemical engineer."

His face fell. After a moment he said, "Well, you can go back to your unit."

Knowing that my future in the army was tenuous, as I was leaving the room I dared to blurt out, "Sir, remember me."

He glanced up and replied, "I will."

I saluted again and left.

To my surprise, about a week later I was suddenly transferred from my regiment at the front to the chemical platoon at brigade headquarters, located about three-quarters of a kilometer behind the front.

Again, the colonel sent for me. He was sitting behind his highly-polished desk, leaning forward in his chair.

"Welcome Yacoub," he said, warmly. "You say you are a chemical engineer?"

"Yes, sir," I replied, standing stiffly at attention.

"Where did you study?"

"At Baghdad University, sir."

"Good grades?"

"Upper quarter of my class, sir."

"And I suppose you received a firm grounding in mathematics and physics?"

"That's right, sir."

"What about English?" he continued.

"Yes, sir, I did study English."

I was becoming more and more perplexed by his questions. No one in the army had ever taken the least interest in my background, as long as I could tote an RPK and follow orders.

He leaned back in his chair, and looked vacantly through me, toying with a pencil. Finally, he said, "Yacoub, my children back at home in Baghdad need a little help with their studies and I need a reliable tutor for them. Do you think you would be capable of teaching them? Math, chemistry, physics, and English?"

Ah, so this was what he was driving at. I relaxed a bit, and smiled. "Yes, sir," I answered, emphatically, "That is no problem at all; I would love to do that!"

From that point on, the colonel sent me on long furloughs—longer than usual—to teach his children in Baghdad. When he went home on furlough he often extended my furloughs even longer, allowing me to spend a lot of time in the capital. Even though both Iraq and Iran had developed long-range surface-to-surface missiles, and were capable of bombing each other's capitals, it was still safer in Baghdad than at the front, where bombs, shells, and bullets showered us day and night.

While I was safely back in the capital, my brigade engaged the Iranians several times, and a number of my comrades were injured and killed. Each time I returned to my unit, the colonel would send me back to Baghdad after two or three days, and whenever he moved to a different unit, he took me with him.

Even so, more than once, on the days I was back with my regiment, I experienced bombing attacks and narrowly avoided being killed.

On one occasion, I left my bunker to buy something at the commissary store. The bunker was protected somewhat because it was on a hillside, but as soon as I got to the main road I was exposed. The road had a berm along one side and a flat, open field on the other. I heard the release of a 106-millimeter Jeep-mounted shell. These shells are highly destructive because of their incredible power and speed. I barely had time to lie down, falling onto the angle of the berm with my body still exposed to shell fragments and my head in a vulnerable position.

The shell fell about fifty meters from me, and I was sure I had breathed my last. I could hear the shrapnel piercing the hillsides round about and was waiting to be sliced up at any moment. My head, being higher than the rest of my body, was especially vulnerable.

I prayed, saying joyfully, "O Jesus, I am coming, Jesus!" I was overwhelmed with such peace that I didn't care what might happen to me. Unbelievably, not one bit of shrapnel hit me. I got up, intending to run, but then a second shell was launched. "O, my God!" All I had time to do was drop to the road and lie flat.

As I prayed, I was again filled with a deep peace. I was surrounded by sparkling stars and heard soft, musical chimes in the distance. Again, I was untouched. This time I got up and sprinted back to my bunker. Several of my comrades had been watching from their bunkers and were surprised to see that I had lived through the attack.

Around this time, Colonel Qais was promoted to General. He was a pious Muslim, a good, God-fearing believer. He believed the Qur'an taught that God had measured the lifespan of each person beforehand and preordained the number of their days. He lived by the maxim, "Our times are in God's hand." Because he had faith in God's timing, he was not afraid of the bombings. He wouldn't even duck his head during attacks, despite flying shrapnel. During one military offensive he was standing out in the open exploring the situation with the commander of another brigade while the bombing was going on. He told his bodyguards to crouch down and watch out for shrapnel. He, however, stood watching, prayer beads in hand.

When he was given command of the Al-Farouk Troops of the Seventh Corps in Basra, he transferred me to his personal bodyguard platoon. It was during this time that the bunker we were in received a direct hit. Fortunately the roof held, or else we would have been crushed to death.

Later, General Qais was transferred to the capital, and he arranged for me to be transferred to the PSCC Regiment (Protection and Services of Command Centers Regiment) in Baghdad. This regiment had outposts throughout the country. Later I was transferred for a time to one of these outposts.

I continued to teach his children for about four years, but once I moved to Baghdad the lessons stopped and I never saw him again. In our last encounter I presented him with a Bible, for which he thanked me.

I was thankful to God for the way he protected me over the years. From the time I started teaching the general's children until the end of the war, I saw much less suffering and agony. Being stationed in Baghdad, I used my newfound freedom to get involved in my church's activities, especially the youth group, Akhawiya.

God has a way of changing the course of our lives when we least expect it. While throwing myself into church and youth group activities, I met a remarkable person who would have an enormous impact on the rest of my life.

12

FINDING A PARTNER

My parents repeatedly suggested that I get to know one or another of their well-off acquaintances, hoping I would marry one of them. To them, making a good catch meant marrying someone who was rich and influential. Although they meant well, I did not want to follow that route. I was determined that I would not accept an arranged marriage—common in my culture—but find a girl who loved me and whom I loved. More than that, I wanted to marry a Christian girl, a girl who was devoted to God and actively serving him.

I grew up in a broken home and suffered from it all my life, so I was determined to find a godly partner who would remain faithful to me "until death do us part." For me, divorce was never an option because of the bitter fruits I had harvested in my childhood.

There were several young women in Akhawiya, but I wasn't especially attracted to any of them. I prayed that

God would direct me to the woman who was ordained to be my life partner, and then I left the matter in his capable hands.

One day after an Akhawiya activity, I was standing on the balcony of one of the buildings in the church compound, talking to a young woman who was new to the youth group. Her name was Layla, and I immediately noticed that she spoke with the same peculiar accent as my family. She must be from the Mosul region, I thought.

She was lithe and slim, with brown shoulder-length curls, intense dark green eyes and an infectious smile. I was attracted by her quiet, sober character, but when she asked me a simple question—"*wesab?*" (where?)—I was totally smitten. Somehow I knew in my heart at that moment that this was the girl I would marry.

After that I was constantly thinking about her, but I didn't give her any indication of my feelings, though I often saw her in church and in youth group whenever I was home on furlough.

After a few months, I got up enough courage to ask Bushra, one of Layla's friends in Akhawiya, to tell her that I wanted to marry her.

Layla retorted, "If he wants to marry me he will have to come ask my mother." Her father had died some years before.

I wanted my parents to come with me to ask for her

hand, but my stepmother refused, convinced that I had already gone to see Layla's family with Nana.

"Why should we come along with you?" she asked, bitterly. "You and your grandmother already went behind our backs!"

However much I tried to persuade her that I had not gone with Nana, she would not believe me, so I finally went alone, just to get acquainted with Layla's family.

Layla's mother, Warena, seemed to be open to my proposition, but she had two important stipulations. First of all, she insisted I finish my university studies before thinking of marriage and, secondly, that next time I come with my parents.

I was crestfallen. This was 1987, and I still hadn't taken those two final exams to get my degree. It meant that we would have to wait a year or more before we could marry. I didn't have any choice, however, because this was Mama's decree!

Layla worked as a secretary and accountant for a construction firm, and I used to call her at her office almost every day. We also often saw each other after church or in our youth group.

It took me a year, but I finally passed my exams—with flying colors. Since the storm had passed, my stepmother agreed at last to go with me and Baba to ask for Layla's hand. We drove the ten or so minutes from our house to Layla's in the Al-Amin Al-Ula district by the Army Canal and were warmly invited in by Layla's mother and six siblings—three sisters and three brothers.

Since Layla was sitting in the living room with her youthful mother and three sisters, my poor father looked bewilderingly from one woman to another.

"Which one is Layla?" he whispered in English.

I whispered back, also in English, "The one with the dress that has a pattern of small flowers."

Baba came straight to the point. "Sister Warena, our son Yacoub would like to marry your Layla."

I had high hopes that we could be immediately engaged, but those hopes were dashed when her mother said, "Please give us a week to think about it." Since we were not related, and since our families did not know each other, Layla's mother wanted to be prudent and learn a bit more about our background.

Optimistic and hopeful, I left with my parents.

During that week, which seemed endlessly long, Layla's mother checked up on us, especially conferring with our local priest Father Phillip Helayi, who had known my family for many years. He was the one to whom I confessed my sins when I turned my life around in 1983, and he had noticed a radical change in my life since then. When Warena asked him what he thought about her daughter marrying me, he replied, "If I had a daughter, I would give her to him in marriage."

Ya Salam, what a wonderful answer!

So, Layla's mother returned home reassured. When we went to see her again at the end of the week, she offered us Arabic coffee. According to Iraqi custom, if she gave us leave to drink the coffee, we would know that her response was positive, so Baba asked, discreetly, "Shall we drink the coffee?"

"Yes, you may drink it." Layla's mother replied.

Whew! We had permission to get engaged!

We started right away to prepare for our engagement. According to Middle Eastern tradition, the bridegroom was expected to buy gold accessories for the bride— rings, arm bands, bracelets, and necklaces. Layla and I went with my stepmother and her mother to the gold market in the Al-Jadeeda district, where we purchased the necessary items. We also bought her a new dress for the occasion.

It was customary for the bride's family to hold the engagement party. Since they invited all their relatives, and we invited all of ours, they had to open a sliding door between the sitting room and the guest room to accommodate the huge crowd. Father Phillip Helayi was also invited.

We danced line dances, threading our way from one room to another. Some of the children played outside in their garden, and some in the side street. Tables were laden with every imaginable Iraqi delicacy: maqlooba, dolma (stuffed grape leaves), kibbeh, tabouli salad, pota-to-chaab, and kibbit-halab.

The women burst forth in waves of ululation—*halahil*— when my parents brought in the gold jewelry and put it on Layla. Someone took handfuls of tiny, paper-wrapped chocolates and tossed them over us, while the children scrambled to collect them.

Then Father Phillip Helayi told us to take each other's hands. When we had done so, he laid his hands on ours and said a prayer, after which he pronounced a blessing. After the blessing, he explained to us that the engagement period is meant to be a time for us to deepen our relationship. He stressed the importance of keeping Christ in the center of our relationship during this time.

Finally, the engagement cake arrived and, as seems to be the custom everywhere, we had to cut it and feed one another. Despite the war, we were very happy.

Over the next days, I visited Layla's home often and went out with her family on picnics and visits. My parents took us once to an Indian restaurant on the seventeenth floor of a building on Abu Nawas Street, by the Tigris River. The air conditioning created a deliciously cool atmosphere, while the elevation gave us a breathtaking 360-degree view of the city. Another time Layla and I went to Zawraa's Tower restaurant.

These were unforgettable days. Layla's large extended family was close-knit and celebrated beautiful traditions. Members of her family often invited us to visit them, at which times they prepared festive dinners, replete with Iraqi delicacies, like kibbeh and dolma and pacha.

Once while I was on a drive with Layla, I said to her, "May I ask you a very important question?"

"Yes, what is it?"

"I need an answer right now, before we get married, otherwise we will have to end our relationship."

Layla was understandably surprised and asked in a tense voice, "Well, okay, what is your question?"

"You know," I began, "one day I might study for the priesthood and dedicate the rest of my life to serving the church. Can you accept that?" (Eastern Catholic churches allow married men to become priests.)

Layla relaxed and smiled. She replied, simply, "Yes, I can accept that. It is also important to me that as true believers we serve Christ."

My joy knew no bounds, and I felt flushed upon hearing her answer.

From that time on we started buying furnishings for our new home. This was the responsibility of the bridegroom, while providing the bride's clothes and linen was the responsibility of the bride's family. We started buying furniture and whatever we needed for our house. Nana had an empty flat in her house, which she offered to let us use free of charge.

We did not set a date for the wedding, since we did not know how long it would take us to prepare our new home. But we did use the time to deepen our relationship, as Father Phillip Helayi had enjoined us to do. The more I learned about Layla, her family, and her origins, the more I marveled at God's grace and unfathomable wisdom. He had chosen the perfect bride for me.

13

LAYLA

But who was this girl I was about to marry? As we got to know each other better, she told me about her youth and growing up, her family, and her ancestry.

Her forebears came from Sirnak province, in southeastern Turkey not far from the northern border of Iraq, and had lived in that region for many generations. Her tribe was probably made up of remnants of the Assyrians and Chaldeans who took refuge in the remote, rugged areas in search of safety after the fall of their empires 2,600 years previously.

The village her family came from was called Hoz, and her clan was called Hozi or Hoznayi in Chaldean. At one time Layla's great-grandfather, Yousif, was the mayor of the village Hoz. His wife's name was Shemmamye. The family had extensive agricultural lands, with gardens, livestock, and beehives. They spoke Chaldean, or Assyrian, which is similar to the Aramaic language that was spoken in the time of Christ.

During the early part of the twentieth century, many Christian groups were persecuted by the Turks and the Kurds, as the government was weak and there was no security net or legal system to protect them during the time of the Ottoman aghas. Layla's grandfather told her stories, often with tears flowing down his cheeks, about the persecution they suffered. Despite the persecution and forced migration, he said they were always happy because Jesus was in their hearts. "They cannot take Him away from us," he would say. "He is with us wherever we are and wherever they send us."

To humiliate the Christian men, the Kurds would raid their villages at night and abduct their wives, bragging to the husbands, "They're our wives now, not yours!"

There is a famous story from that time of a young woman, newly married, named Mariam Al-Hozi, a relative of Layla's grandparents. In 1913 Tammer Ibin Osman, the son of a Kurdish agha, once came from a neighboring village and noticed Mariam milking sheep in the field, along with a group of girls. He approached Mariam, and ordered her, in front of the other girls, to follow him so he could marry her. The man was a Muslim, so this meant that Mariam would be forced to deny her faith in Jesus, as well as commit adultery.

She refused.

He threatened her saying, "Don't you know that I can kill you at this very moment?"

She answered, "Be that as it may, it is better for me to die in my faith in Jesus than to follow you into apostasy."

He grabbed her and lifted her onto his back by force, but she resisted, hitting him on the head. Struggling, she got free and started screaming, but he was so infuriated that he raised his dagger and stabbed her several times in the abdomen, killing her instantly. Suddenly, a light streamed down from the sky, and her body was illuminated with a white radiance. Tammer Ibin Osman was so overcome by fear and dread that he took flight.

The people of the village sent a message to the bishop of Zakho about Mariam Al-Hozi's martyrdom. The bishop studied the possibility of building a shrine, and her grave became a place of pilgrimage. Christians from the neighboring villages took soil from the ground surrounding her grave to take home for healing. The bishop instructed the people to keep a small bowl of water on the grave, so that anyone who was sick could drink from it and be healed. Legend has it that many were healed.

Due to mounting persecution against the Christians during the First World War, the people of Hoz, as well as the surrounding villages, were forced to flee, preventing the building of the shrine. Layla's great-grandfather, Yousif, trekked with part of the clan through rugged mountains to northern Iraq, where a lot of his people suffered and died—especially killed by bears in the mountains. Both of Layla's paternal grandparents were killed by bears, after which Layla's father was taken in by his older brother, who was already married.

As a result of the chaos during their flight, Yousif got separated from his wife, Shemmamye, for a time.

She, along with another group, migrated to Russia. Other groups migrated to France. After a long time, Shemmamye found out where he was and was able to join him and the family in northern Iraq. They settled in the town of Zakho near the Turkish border.

Layla was born in that region, in the village of Shekaftmara, on Saturday, the sixth of January 1962. Three years later the family moved to Mahalat Al-Nasara.

When she was six years old, her family moved to the city of Mosul, where she grew up, assimilating the new culture around her. After her grandparents' family moved from Zakho to Baghdad, her grandmother, Wardye, a God-fearing woman, asked if Layla could live with her in Baghdad. This way she would be closer to a church youth group, since in Mosul Layla's family lived very far from any churches.

Several years later Layla's family bought a house in Baghdad, in the same area where I lived, so the whole family moved to Baghdad and Layla joined her family there. Layla started attending the same local church and youth group that I attended.

14

NO MORE WAR

The PSCC regiment had an outpost in Basra—one of the better assignments to which General Qais had transferred me. During my engagement I was reassigned there, but I took my furloughs in Baghdad. In order to get back home more often, a lance corporal and I used to cover for each other, taking turns going secretly to Baghdad.

Each time I went home, I gave my firearm to a fellow soldier for safekeeping, without going through the formal channels. But once while I was in Baghdad, the gun disappeared. No one seemed to know what had happened to it.

An investigation board initiated a formal charge against me, because I was the owner of the gun. The supervisor in charge of the inquiry found me guilty, while using the soldier who lost the gun as a witness.

This was a great shock, especially since I was innocent, and the other soldier was guilty. However, one of my friends worked in the office and managed to revise the file at the last minute, reversing our roles. I was now the witness and the other soldier the guilty party.

I was summoned to a military board, but the board was repeatedly postponed, because the other soldier never showed up. In the end I managed to get off the hook. If I had been found guilty, I would probably have had to spend at least six months in prison, and then serve an additional year and a half in the army!

On the 20th of August 1988, one and a half months into our engagement, I was on furlough, spending the evening with Layla at her home. At about eleven o'clock I said goodbye and went home to try to get some sleep. Around midnight Baba woke me up all excited.

"Yacoub, Yacoub!" he shouted, shaking me awake.

Bleary-eyed I looked up at him. "What's the matter?"

"Wake up, wake up! The war is over! Come, see what's on TV!"

I jumped out of bed, hardly daring to believe what he was saying and watched, incredulous, the TV news report. After eight years of war, hundreds of thousands of deaths and untold destruction, Iraq and Iran had finally agreed to a ceasefire brokered by the United Nations. The two countries were going to start direct negotiations.

I hurried outside to Baba's car and drove back to Layla's house, waking the whole household.

"The war is over," I told them, jubilantly.

Then I took them all with me in the car and we drove through the streets of Baghdad at one o'clock in the morning, where the people were already partying. Iraqis had long ago lost hope that this interminable, destructive war would ever end, so they could hardly believe that peace had come. They banged metal pots on their terraces, out of their windows and on their balconies. They filled the streets, dancing and singing, and throwing water on cars. The streets were jammed with traffic, horns were blaring and riders were shouting their joy and relief. Those who had guns were shooting them in the air.

Baghdad did not sleep that night. The people's longing for peace was fulfilled.

15

MARRIAGE

I was transferred from Basra back to the regimental headquarters in Baghdad during the time of my engagement. I was quartered in a barracks and could only go home every other day, because of extended duties. But to my surprise, two days before our wedding I was reassigned to an office in the Defense Ministry, allowing me to go home at four o'clock every day, with no additional duties. That was a present from heaven.

When I arrived at my new office on the first day, I immediately turned in a request to my supervisor for a ten-day wedding furlough.

"Well, well," he said, smiling. "You haven't even started working yet, and you're asking for a vacation!"

I grinned back at him. "Yes, but look here," I explained, showing him a fistful of cards and brochures. "See, here is our wedding invitation. The wedding is this Saturday. And we have booked and paid for everything—the church, the club, the hotel, and everything else. We've sent out all our invitations..."

"Ok, ok, I'm not going to stand in the way," he said, as he smiled and shook my hand vigorously. "We wish you many blessings. Here, let me sign the request, so you can take it to General Saad, the manager of the office."

Several of my Akhawiya friends pitched in to help with wedding preparations. Through a pilot, the fiancé of a young woman in Akhawiya, we were able to rent the Military Officers Cultural Centre in the Zayouna district of Baghdad. Another friend offered to film the wedding. The sister of my friend Emad worked in a flower shop, and promised to make us a beautiful bouquet. The band we hired was lively, and was managed by two young brothers, Saher and Wesam. Because these goods and services were procured through Akhawiya friends, they cost about half of what they normally would have. In addition, our church only asked for a token fee.

Furthermore, since the cost of living dropped dramatically at the end of the hostilities with Iran, we were able to furnish our new home for half of what it would have cost during the war. The cost of Layla's wedding dress and my black suit also dropped considerably.

Other friends also helped us. One of Layla's business friends, Olivia, whose uncle owned a bakery, ordered us a *ten-tier* wedding cake—for next to nothing. Our next-door Muslim neighbor, Jwad, wanted to hire a mobile music band to play music during the drive through Baghdad on our wedding day. These bands, made up of trumpet, snare, bass drum, and cymbals, were usually in one of the cars following the vehicle transporting the wedding party and blasted music at full volume out of their open windows.

I politely declined his offer, but asked him whether we could use his 500SEL Mercedes as a wedding car. He was delighted to let us use it and even drove us himself. At his own expense, he had the car decorated with streamers and ribbons.

On the wedding day, the fifteenth of October 1988, it rained for the first time that fall. The club phoned to ask if I wanted the reception indoors or out. I thought for a moment and, taking the risk, said, "Outdoors!" I guessed right, because although the day was a bit nippy, it didn't rain—neither during the ceremony nor during the reception.

My family and I went to Layla's house to receive Layla from her eldest brother Nashwan. Of course, all the family and neighbors were raising a hubbub with their ululations. From there we headed toward the church, driving in a long procession.

The ceremony took place in the Mar Behnam Church in the Al-Ghadeer district of Baghdad. Father Raphael Kotaimy,* assisted by Father Yousif Shalita, married us. Apart from our relatives and church friends, the members

---

* Father Raphael Kotaimy received a severe back wound in 2010 during a terrorist attack on his church, Our Lady of Salvation Church. This attack claimed the lives of dozens of worshipers. Later, Pope Francis met him in an intimate historical encounter.

of two Akhawiya groups–the Holy Family Church in Sa'doun and the Mar Elia Church–attended the wedding.

Traditionally two witnesses accompany the couple during the wedding service, the *qareeb* (best man) for the groom, and the *qareeba* (maid of honor) for the bride.* The witnesses sign the church registry. During the ceremony, the priest asked us the marriage questions, including the question about being faithful to each other until death. He then gave us rings, saying a prayer for each of us as we put them on each other.

After the wedding, Layla, the *qareeb*, the *qareeba* and I went to Pack Studio, one of the best photo studios in Iraq, to have wedding pictures taken. Hazim Pack, the owner, was a relative.

We arrived at the club around eight o'clock in the evening and were met by a big crowd of people–family, relatives, friends, and associates–who were dancing in front of us as we entered the club and proceeded to the reception garden. The band was already in place, playing Arabic, Assyrian, and Western love songs. My stepmother walked just ahead of Layla and me, sprinkling rose water all over us from a special conical pitcher.

Waiters served sandwiches, drinks, and cake, while the guests continued dancing around the dance floor for hours. As was the custom, many of our friends and relatives came by to greet us, pressing envelopes with money into our palms to help us set up our new household.

---

* Iraqi Christians in the United States have expanded this to seven men and seven women, all dressed alike.

Around one o'clock in the morning, Layla and I finally slipped away to our waiting car, accompanied by our immediate families. It had been a joyful time, but we were exhausted, not only from the festivities, but from the strain of preparing for the engagement and wedding. And there had been so many obstacles in our way over the preceding years! We were grateful that now that was all in the past, and we could go forward and found our new family.

For our honeymoon, we went to Hotel Babylon in the Karrada district on the Tigris, staying on the thirteenth floor. Our room faced the beautiful orchards there.

Returning home we continued celebrating with our relatives, visiting back and forth for days. It felt like our wedding was part of a larger national outburst of joy, celebrating the end of the war. I think the guests at our wedding dove into the festivities with more than the usual vigor, happy that the country was finally at peace.

A great burden had been lifted from the soul of the Iraqi people, and the relief was palpable. What would happen now? Would the people finally learn to live in true peace with one another?

16

MARIAM

A couple of months later, to our horror, Nana was suddenly struck with terminal cancer, and life became hectic. Since we lived with her, we were able to give her daily care. Aunt Victoria came from Lebanon with her son Tony to be with her mother in those difficult days.

We once asked Nana, during her illness, if we could bring a priest, so she could confess her sins and be anointed with oil in the name of the Lord. She agreed, as she was in great pain. We used to give her so many analgesic tablets that she couldn't stand up anymore, and then we would have to carry her to the car and drive her to the hospital for injections. But the pain was unabated.

To our amazement, after she confessed her sins to the priest and he prayed over her, all the pain disappeared. Her cancer still progressed from day to day, but she never had to take painkillers again. In her last days she was very peaceful.

Shortly after we were married we discovered, to our joy, that we were going to have a baby! We decided to call the baby Faadi, which means "redeemer" in Arabic, if it was a boy or Mariam, after the Virgin Mary, if it was a girl.

As the time of the birth approached, Layla had to go to the hospital for regular check-ups. On the tenth of August, 1989, during one of these examinations, the doctor, an Armenian, found that Layla had very high blood pressure. She told her to hurry home to pack her clothes and come straight back to the hospital. Layla phoned her mother, who came immediately to our house and went together with her to the Al Alwaiya Maternity Hospital in the Karadah district. She also phoned her workplace to tell them that it might be a couple of days before she could return to work.

Upon arriving at the hospital, Layla was immediately taken into surgery. Because of the danger due to her high blood pressure, the doctor had to perform an emergency caesarean section.

Layla's mother waited anxiously, offering up fervent prayers. Around the middle of the afternoon, a nurse hurried out of the delivery room, carrying a little bundle, and headed down the corridor.

Seeing the concerned look on Layla's mother's face, the nurse announced, "It's a girl!"

The baby was taken immediately to intensive care and given oxygen, because she was having some breathing difficulties. Layla's mother was very concerned, but the nurses comforted her and told her not to worry, as this often happens, and the baby would most likely be all right.

After the delivery, Layla was taken to a ward, but soon had a convulsion and lost consciousness. Her mother rushed frantically to a nurse and exclaimed, "My daughter is dying. Come and help!"

The nurse hurried to Layla's side and explained that this is sometimes a normal reaction to high blood pressure, but they expected her to stabilize.

The baby recovered and was brought into the ward, where she was placed in Layla's arms, even though she was still unconscious. During this time, her mother had to look after the baby.

I knew nothing of what was happening, as I was at work all day, and it was almost impossible to contact me. I only found out when I arrived home at around five in the evening. I immediately grabbed a bag of baby clothes and headed straight for the hospital, not knowing what to expect.

When I arrived and entered Layla's ward, I saw her lying in bed, just opening her eyes. Her mother was sitting next to her with the baby in her arms. What an incredible feeling! God had given us a child. I was overwhelmed, as I slowly approached them.

Layla's mother said, "It is a girl."

"Wow, a girl!" I exclaimed in awe. "Mariam."

Layla's mother handed me the baby and as I took the little bundle in my arms, I wept for joy, gazing for many minutes at this perfect little creature–this gift from heaven.

Layla had to stay in the hospital for ten days, until she had fully recovered and the doctors were reassured that there were no further adverse effects. During this time, her mother stayed at her side day and night.

When I returned home in the evening after the birth, I told my aunt and my grandmother the good news. My grandmother was struggling to breathe, because the cancer had spread to her chest. She was lying flat on her bed.

I whispered in her ear, "Nana, I have a new baby, a little girl. Her name is Mariam."

She nodded, looking all the while at the ceiling.

"Are you not going to give us a blessing?" I asked.

With a great deal of effort, she mumbled, "*Embarek*," which means congratulations or blessings.

What a joy and privilege to hear my grandmother's blessing. She was the one who had brought me up after my parents divorced and until Baba remarried when I was ten years old. She meant the world to me.

Two days after Mariam's birth, Nana passed away.

17

LET ME OUT!

Being good Catholics we had our baby baptized when she was forty days old by Father Philip Helayi at Mar Ilia Al-Heri Church. Many friends and relatives attended the ceremony, and we had a celebration afterwards.

Mariam was blond like my mother, but with dark green eyes like Layla and me. She was loved very much by both relatives and neighbors. Many times we had to ask, "Where is Mariam?" because Layla's two youngest sisters frequently whisked her away to show her around the neighborhood. They treated her like one of their little dolls.

Now that the war was over and I had a growing family, I was more anxious than ever to be free from the regimentation and hypocrisy of army life. We had seen intense suffering over the previous years. One of my relatives, Ra'eef Muneer, was a master swordsman. After forty days at the front, he was shot in the chest and died, leaving behind a fiancée. He was supposed to have gone to Cuba to represent Iraq in an international sporting event. He was so well-known that the fencing hall in the Physical Education Faculty of Baghdad University was named after him—the Martyr Ra'eef Hall.

Layla's family suffered much more. Three brothers from the same family—cousins of Layla's mother—were killed, two in the Iran war, and the third later, during the Kuwait conflict.

So I was happy that the government began to discharge soldiers soon after the end of hostilities with Iran.

Kais Abbo, an Akhawiya friend, and I decided to open a women's clothing store in a brand-new mall near the Technology University to increase our income. We were in a poor location, so the store did not do well. To be able to meet the rent payments I had to start playing drums again with a band in one of the discotheques. But this didn't set well with my conscience. In the end, we had to sell the store and I quit the band.

My age group came up for discharge in early 1990, after I had been in the army for well over eight years—more than six years over the normal twenty-three-month enlistment. Besides losing most of my youth to the war, my career had stalled, since I could not get any experience in my field of chemical engineering. Still, I was glad to get out in one piece.

I went from my office in the Defense Ministry to the personnel office of the PSCC regiment to apply for a discharge, ecstatic to be leaving the horrors of military life behind. But the personnel officer was decidedly not happy. In fact, he looked downright gloomy. Like many officers, he had joined the army for life during the war years to receive the incredible perks and privileges that officers enjoyed. Now that the war had ended and the draftees were being discharged, he resented that we would be free while he was stuck in the army for the rest of his life. I could see the resentment in his eyes.

I filled out the necessary forms and then left the office, my spirits high. The next day I went back to see if my application had been approved. When I walked into the office, the personnel officer was standing behind the counter.

"Sir," I began, "I would like to check on the progress of my discharge application."

Going to a file cabinet, he pulled out my service record and returned to the counter. "I have bad news for you. You're being charged with desertion."

"Desertion?" I nearly exploded. "How can..."

"It says here in your records that when you were drafted, you disappeared after leaving the recruiting center and did not show up for duty until five days later. If you had been away for less than five days, you would only have had to spend two days in the brig for each day you were AWOL. But five days is considered desertion."

"But that's absurd. I wasn't officially signed up until I showed up for duty. I can't be charged with desertion; I was still a civilian."

"That's the law," he insisted. "Five days' absence constitutes desertion. I'm sending your file to an investigative board, and if you're found guilty you'll be sentenced to at least six months in prison and have to spend an additional year in the army."

I wanted to argue with him, but I had sense enough to hold my tongue. I was shocked and dumbfounded. How could he do that to me? It was totally unjust, and I suspected he was going after me because he was stuck in the army while I was getting out.

I was devastated. I had given eight years and three months of my life to my country and now the army was doing this to me? I had been so jubilant about getting a discharge. Layla and I could build our home, I could finally get on with my career, and we would have the freedom to do what we wanted without the restrictions—and dangers—of the army hanging over our heads. Oh God, what should I do?

I went to the regiment commander to see if he could resolve the issue in my favor, but he told me the personnel officer knew more about it than he did, so his hands were tied.

At that point I was desperate. I decided to go over his head and see General Saad, commander-in-chief of PSCC Regiment. He had more authority, and was the administrator of the office where I worked. He knew me well, because I had worked for a year and a half in his office. I walked into his office and explained the situation to him in detail.

After listening to my woeful tale, he said, "Don't worry, I'll take care of it. In fact," he added, reaching for his phone, "hang on a minute, and I'll see what I can do right now."

He dialed a number and then waited for an answer. After a moment, he said, "Hello, this is General Saad. You have a soldier named Yacoub Yousif in your regiment. He's having a bit of a problem with his separation. The personnel office is claiming he deserted because he didn't appear for duty until five days after he registered at the recruiting center, but he was still a civilian during those five days. I hope that you can push his discharge papers through."

I could just hear the tinny voice of the person at the other end of the line saying, "Yes, sir, right away! Send him back to the office and we'll take care of everything."

I breathed a sigh of relief, thanking the general and wishing him God's blessings. Then I rushed back to the PSCC personnel office.

To my surprise, the personnel officer was quite jovial, when I entered the office this time. He handed me the dossier containing my service record and the official document signed by the regiment commander that would allow my final discharge to be processed and wished me luck. I held the file to my chest, hardly believing that I would soon be a free man.

As I was leaving my regiment complex I turned and looked back at the unit. It felt like I was being released from prison, and I gave a sigh of relief. "I will never have to see you or the army again," I thought. "I am leaving you forever! No more slavery!"

How wrong I was. . . .

18

COMPLICATIONS

I hailed a taxi and went to the local Army Recruiting Center, where my discharge needed to be recorded in my Military Service Book, the official record that citizens had to carry at all times to prove they had served in the military.

The office was on the third floor. When I arrived at the building, I was dismayed to see that the line of soldiers waiting to be discharged stretched all the way down to the main street. There was no ventilation inside the building, and in spite of the fact that it was February, the building was hot and stuffy. When I arrived at the head of the line, after a two-hour wait, there was nothing in front of me but a blank wall.

"Where is the window to turn in my application?" I asked a soldier near me.

"Down there," he said, pointing down toward the base of the wall.

I looked down, and saw that the window was very low to accommodate the clerk seated at a desk on the other side—with no consideration for the soldiers who had to double up in order to talk through the window. I felt silly bowing and putting half of my body through the window in order to talk to the clerk.

He took my dossier, and said, "Come back tomorrow."

Ah, I will be free tomorrow, I thought. I returned the next day, again waiting in the long queue. When I finally arrived at the window, the clerk told me, "Oh, we can't release you."

"Huh, why not?" I asked, heatedly.

"You'll have to go back to your unit and get your application corrected. We can't process your papers, because there is a word missing in your application."

What?" I exclaimed. "What's missing?"

Pointing to a paper, he said, "It says here that the discharge decision came from the President. They didn't write Mr. President. The word "Mr." is missing."

I almost lost it and had to bite my tongue to keep from bellowing at the clerk. I forced myself to be polite, and said, "Ok, let me go and get it corrected."

They transferred me back to my unit, with a document requesting the correction. I took the application back to my regiment, which I had hoped to never see again, and asked a clerk there to add the missing word. They hurriedly fixed the omission and gave me a document transferring me back to the center. Of course, I had to wait in the same long line. Arriving for the third time at the window, I handed the discharge application to a clerk, who told me to come back the next day.

When I got to the head of the line the next day, the clerk told me that before I could submit my application, I had to get it approved at the Al-Rusafa recruiting center on the eastern side of the Tigris—all the way on other side of town.

Good Lord, when would this run-around ever end?

I took a taxi to the office that was located in the Al-Adhamiyah district of Baghdad. This was the main Army Recruiting Center, housed in a simple villa in Al-Rusafa. The entrance was in the back of the building, so I had to pass through the garage, into a garden, and around the back of the villa to where a line of soldiers was waiting.

But now a most bizarre scene met my eyes. The office window through which the soldiers had to pass their files was more than two yards above the ground. A row of bricks at chest height protruded out about four inches from the wall. Several soldiers were perched on the brick ledge, facing the wall with hands outstretched to keep from falling. They were inching their way closer and closer to the window, with their papers dangling between their lips. They were hot and sweaty from balancing on the wall in the sun.

As each one approached the window, he bent down—because now the window was at his waist level—and handed the papers through. When he was finished, he had to jump off the ledge into a pool of mud, created by a tap where the parched soldiers could get a drink of water after their balancing act.

I took my place in the precarious line on the wall and, when my turn came, handed my papers through the window.

"Come back tomorrow," I heard the clerk say. Why didn't that surprise me!

The next day I went through the same wall gymnastics. This time, my application was ready. I grabbed it, jumped down into the mud and hurried away, happy to have my completed application—in spite of the splotches of mud on my trousers.

I returned to the local third-floor center and handed over my application, expecting to hear the usual "come back tomorrow."

But, no. "Come back in a month," the clerk said. "Your military book should be signed and ready by then."

I finally felt confident that I would be discharged soon and was keen to begin a career as a chemical engineer. I went to Baba, who was a commercial expert in a brewery and had many trade connections.

"Baba, I'll be out of the army in a month, and I have to find a job in Baghdad as soon as possible."

"Okay, go see Farooq Hunnah in the Pepsi-Cola factory. I think he can find something for you. Tell him you are Yousif's son."

The next day I went to the factory and introduced myself to Farooq, who took me immediately to the general manager's office.

Amazingly, I was hired on the spot, but the manager sent me to the personnel office to take care of the paperwork.

The personnel officer asked me if I had been released from the army.

"Yes, I'm done with my military service."

"Can you please bring me your Service Book when you have the time?"

I knew I would have it in a month, so I assured him I would bring it in soon. He must have forgotten about it, because he never asked me again. I felt greatly relieved; I was out—well *almost* out—of the army, and I already had a steady job. Things were looking up.

When the month was over, I returned to my recruiting center.

An officer was sitting at a desk, working. "I've come for my Service Book, sir," I said.

Glancing up at me, he said, "I don't know where it is!"

"I was told it would be signed and ready..."

Turning to the right, he pointed toward a heap of papers in the corner of the room. "Take a look over there," he said. "Maybe you'll find what you need in that pile."

For the first time in a month, I was overcome with uncertainty. What if the book wasn't there, after all?

I crouched down and began rummaging through the mound of books on the floor, checking each one to see if it bore my name. After a couple of minutes, I found a book with the inscription "Yacoub Yousif." Wonder of wonders, a book with my name! I leafed through the book a couple of times, just to make sure that it was really mine, checking that it had the crucial signature. Yes, there it was. Hugging the book to my chest, I mumbled my thanks and hurried out of the office.

This book is still valuable to me, and I have kept it ever since.

I went home and celebrated with my wife and family and friends. At long last, after so many years, I was finally free! I was thankful to be able to get out with neither physical nor emotional injuries. Many of my comrades, like hundreds of thousands of other Iraqi citizens, were either dead or scarred for life, and thousands more were still prisoners of war in Iran. I did have occasional bouts of depression, but so did the entire nation—and little wonder, after all those years of carnage.

Above all, I was thankful that I had never been forced to kill another person, although I felt that my reluctance to make a bold witness for peace in the army was the coward's way out.

Even though I was now free of my military shackles, I occasionally worried about the future. Yes, I was out, but was I really free forever?

19

AGITATION ON THE HOME FRONT

After my discharge in 1990, I dreamed of a quiet, peaceful life and started thinking about the future of the family. One thing I wanted to do was to build a house of our own. We even drew up plans together. I probably could have moved to a high-paying job outside of Baghdad in the petroleum or phosphate industries, but I wanted to stay in the capital, close to the church and its activities, as well as our social life.

As in society in general, the Pepsi Cola factory was riddled with class differences, bribery, nepotism, and compromises of all kinds. Only engineers, managers, and office staff received free transportation to and from work. All workers received free meals, but the professional staff dined in their own cafeteria, separated by a glass wall from the blue-collar workers. I detested this segregation and, although I was on the engineering staff, I used to eat with the common workers, which caused me some embarrassment, because of the stares I got from both sides of the wall.

As a consequence of the war, it was almost impossible to procure many parts and ingredients for the manufacture of various products in our country. For instance, I saw a maintenance engineer in the Pepsi plant replace a valve without a required filter, because the filter was unavailable. There were many such infractions in our plant. The quality of this popular drink dropped radically, and eventually I no longer dared to drink Pepsi produced in Iraq, although it had always been one of my favorite beverages.

As for social life, we enjoyed a pleasant relationship with relatives, friends, and neighbors, regardless of their religion. Most neighbors were either Christian or Muslim, but we did have a Jewish couple on our street, Haroon and Daisy, who were loved by all. We also enjoyed going to social clubs and, it goes without saying, to our church activities.

But soon we began to see worrying developments in the country. The army started calling up some of the reservists, as well as soldiers from A-Jaysh A-Sha'bi,* the People's Army. Iraqi troops began to assemble near the Saudi Arabian border. My friends, relatives, and I became more and more alarmed, worried that the country was headed for another war.

---

* The Iraqi Popular Army, also known as the People's Army or People's Militia (A-Jaysh A-Sha'bi), was a paramilitary militia composed of civilian volunteers. The movement developed rapidly over the years, although the soldiers had limited training and were not well equipped. In later years, the numbers in their ranks approached those of the regular armed forces.

Layla and I talked about it. I told her that the very thought of returning to the army frightened me. I would *never* carry a weapon again, regardless of the consequences.

But what could we do? I loved my country, but I loved Jesus more. I knew that army life was incompatible with his commands and that refusing military service would mean death. If I were called up and failed to report I could be executed. Jesus said, "When they persecute you in one town, flee to the next" (Matt. 10:23), so I had no qualms about leaving Iraq. In any case, for the Christian, God's kingdom is our true home.

Now, our dreams of a peaceful, stable family life seemed to be collapsing. We knew that we were faced with some heavy decisions, because everything we had hoped for was now in jeopardy. As we agonized over the issue, we began to feel that the only solution was to leave the country. But where could we go, and how would we get there?

Fortunately, citizens were again given the right to travel abroad—a right that had been denied during the war years. Thousands of people flooded the passport offices in hopes of visiting foreign countries. Many were determined to emigrate without looking back.

I started working night shifts in order to leave my days free to apply for our passports, but this was not easy. The ineptitude and multiple layers of bureaucracy sent me from office to office all over the city to gather the necessary documents.

Once I waited outside an office for two hours in the blazing summer sun, in a line that did not move. Finally, someone went to the front to speak to a clerk.

"Excuse me, brother," he began, "I noticed that the line has not been moving for two hours. Should we continue to wait?"

"Oh, you may as well leave and come back another day," he said. "We ran out of stamps, so we can't process any more documents."

We were dumbfounded. Why hadn't he announced to the people waiting in the intense summer heat that the office was closed?

Because of the night work, I would often be so tired during the day that I could hardly function. One day, I fell asleep for a few seconds at the wheel while driving along a crowded city street. Thank God I didn't get into an accident.

In the meantime, I continued my employment at the Pepsi factory, working in the first of two production halls. Every hall had its own manager and engineers. I noticed after some time that one of the production lines in our hall was at a standstill, even though there were no technical malfunctions. To my dismay, I discovered that our hall manager was skimming workers from the line to do construction and maintenance work on his own house, while the factory was paying their wages.

Once my hall manager was away for a few days, so I wrote up a report about this infraction and submitted it to the manager of the second production hall. He was a Christian with a PhD in chemical engineering who had taken over the duties of my manager during his absence. Almost immediately, he called me into his office.

"What the heck is this about?" he asked, pointing to my report.

"Just what you see," I answered. "It's a report about the corruption in our hall."

He took a fatherly tone. "Yacoub," he began, "I appreciate your honesty, but you will see a lot of things like this in life. The important thing is to work honestly yourself and ignore what others are doing. You can't fix all the world's problems."

"Well," I responded, firmly, "I want to be a good citizen. As such, I have to address problems when I see them."

"But you're only going to get worn out trying to fight the system," he replied. "Do you really want me to sign this and pass it on to the head manager?"

"Yes, please." I replied.

I can't say I hadn't been warned. This manager had experienced the deceit in Iraqi factories for a long time and knew where protesting would lead.

A few days later, as I entered the factory, the managing director, a dark expression on his face, happened to be walking by. With the military spirit so visible in our society, it was not surprising that he had the air of an army commander, with his broad shoulders, bull neck, and hawk eyes.

He stopped in front of me and asked, menacingly, "Are you the engineer named Yacoub?"

"Yes." I replied.

He glared at me with fiery eyes, and shook his head. After he had stared at me for several seconds, he walked away without saying anything.

That weekend, one of my colleagues, who was no more liked than I was, phoned to say that the factory was sending us the following week as inspectors to a remote area of the Diyala district, in order to check up on some of our agents there. It was obvious that this was meant to intimidate us. A task like this was usually relegated to regular staff, not to production engineers.

By way of protest, I didn't go to work at all the following week. This suited me anyway, as I needed time to work on getting a visa to some country that would allow us to immigrate. I was so desperate to leave that I even considered moving to some poor country like Bangladesh.

Three days later my colleague called again to say, "Yacoub, you can come back to the factory. The manager cancelled the inspection job."

When my production manager returned a few days later, he came to me and asked why I had reported him. "Why did you do that to me? I have been sick with worry ever since I heard about it. My blood pressure has gone up and I can't sleep."

"I only did what every good, honest citizen should do," I replied. "I was just reporting something dishonest. Was that wrong?"

He just walked away, shaking his head.

Afterwards, I felt bad wondering if I had done the right thing after all. The proper way of dealing with this situation would have been to go directly to him and challenge him, but instead I had gone over his head. I had not shown him love as a fellow man. Since there was no common ground to deal with such issues, I began to realize that it wouldn't help to criticize my supervisor or any of the people caught up in the net of corruption; they did not know any other way of acting. In any case, Jesus commanded me not to judge others, only myself.

It was clear that what I had seen was not an isolated incident. There was a covert network of corruption and embezzlement throughout the company. I felt that the best thing to do would be to just resign and find another job if I had to, so I submitted my resignation.

My biggest fear was that I might be drafted again into the army, so my main focus was to get a visa to emigrate as soon as possible.

20

A WORLDWIDE SEARCH

When Baba learned about our decision to emigrate, he tried to dissuade us from leaving the country. Once, while we were riding in his car together, he said, "You know, son, if you leave here you're going to be a stranger in a strange land. You won't speak the language and you'll miss your social network. Your academic credentials won't mean a thing, so it will be impossible to find work in your field. Why do you want to leave, when you will be forced to live in such uncertainty and anxiety?"

I tried to explain. "I believe all that, Baba," I replied. "But please try to understand my position. I will refuse to go back to the army if I should be called up, because Jesus forbids killing. You know what will happen to me if I refuse. All I want to do is to follow Jesus without compromise."

But nothing I said convinced him.

"Look," I said. "I'll be happy to work as a cleaner in order to have a clear conscience."

"I just don't understand you," he said.

Turning to him I said, "Do you know that this is all your fault?"

Startled he asked, "What do you mean, my fault? How is it my fault?"

I replied, "You sent me to a Christian elementary school. Here I am now a Christian with the desire to obey Jesus. I do not want to kill."

Shrugging his shoulders, he said, "Well, it's your life, and I won't interfere, but I sure don't understand you."

Layla and I started making the rounds of the foreign embassies in Baghdad to try to get a visa. We soon discovered that we were not the only ones knocking on embassy doors. Thousands of people were converging on them, trying to get visas to—anywhere. People would bring their mattresses with them and camp on the sidewalk outside the embassies, so they could be first in line the next day.

The rush was so disorderly that an Iraqi policeman had to be posted outside the Australian embassy to organize the lines. It was comical to see him there, acting the part of an embassy employee. "This way for tourist visas," he would say, pointing in one direction, "and over there if you're here for immigration."

Of course, there was no way that countries were willing to absorb so many immigrants, and as our search became more frantic, we became more and more disheartened.

Many Iraqis, especially Christians, tried to get visas to Greece because of an organization there that helped

117

refugees. After getting refugee status, this organization would help them relocate to some other country. We planned to take that route if we could get a visa.

Now that Baba realized we were in earnest, he suggested a way he might be able to help us. "Did you ever consider going to Sweden?" he asked once, when we were together.

I didn't know anything about Sweden, but we were desperate to find some escape from Iraq. It didn't really matter to us where we went.

"Sure, why not!" I said. "Why do you ask?"

"Well," he said, "I have a Swedish business friend who might be able to help. Would you like me to talk to him?"

This gave me a glimmer of hope. "Yes, please do."

A few days later I got a letter of invitation from Baba's associate, inviting us to pay a visit to his home in Sweden. He also sent a copy to the Swedish embassy. Immediately after getting the letter, we went to the embassy to apply for the visas.

We returned three days later and, lo and behold, there were the precious visa stickers in our passports. We felt like we were walking on air as we headed toward the door, gazing at the visa stickers in our passports. We could hardly believe we were that much closer to freedom. We could see envy and amazement on the faces of the dozens of people who were waiting in the embassy lobby. As we walked out, we could hear them whispering among themselves, "Look! Look! They got visas!"

In spite of this, I still had my mind focused on Greece. It was a route with which I was already familiar, knowing that many of my compatriots had gone there and received refugee status. From there we could move to a country of our own choosing—with no turning back.

When one of my friends heard that we had Swedish visas, but were still considering going to Greece, he was baffled. "What? You want to go to Greece? Are you crazy? You have visas for Sweden. Go there and seek asylum!"

Of course, we had no idea what hoops we would have to jump through to get asylum, and as far as we were concerned, one country was as good as another. But my friend was right; why look for more trouble, when we already had a way of escape. That decided it: to Sweden we would go.

When we shared with some of our relatives what we had decided, we learned that we had a distant relative in Sweden. Someone even had his phone number, so I called him to tell him we intended to go there to seek asylum. He welcomed us and said he would be happy to help us once we got to his home.

Now it was time to seriously prepare for departure. We bought airline tickets, sold as many of our possessions as we could, and collected the things we wanted to bring with us. Anything we didn't want we left in our house for Baba to deal with.

As we packed our bags, I realized that our three suitcases contained all our worldly possessions. On the advice of my parents, we bought a baby stroller for Mariam.

The day before we traveled, I took a trip to Mosul to say goodbye to my mother and my grandparents. Now we were ready.

Sweden. We didn't know a thing about it—except that the climate was cold, cold, cold. Our local priest, Father Phillip Helayi, had warned us that we would need warm clothes both winter and summer in Sweden. But we had visas, and that meant escape from tyranny.

We didn't dare say farewell to anyone but our closest relatives, because we were afraid that governmental authorities would block our emigration if they found out we were planning never to return.

We would leave the next day, the thirtieth of June 1990. We slept that night with my parents. I needed to shave, but couldn't find a razor blade. My parents were already in bed and I didn't want to disturb them, so I found an old, used blade and quickly shaved.

Big mistake.

21

IRAQI AIRLINES, HERE WE COME

I woke up the next morning with razor rash all over my face. Ouch! Well, at least I would look like a refugee!

Everything was ready for us to leave. We packed our suitcases into Baba's car, and my brother Arkan drove us to the airport at around five in the morning.

Although we had tickets, we didn't have confirmed seats on a plane. We went to the airport anyway, hoping that seats would be available. To our relief, there were places for us, and we were able to board. Sitting in the plane waiting for takeoff, we felt like we were in a dream; we were actually on our way out.

Knowing that we had a lot of big decisions ahead of us, we prayed that God would work out the countless details. To be sure, our future was a big question mark, but we had each other, and we had Jesus. Apart from my distant relative, we didn't know a soul in Sweden.

We took our seats in the plane, Layla next to the window, I in the middle, and a man on my right.

121

Ten-month-old Mariam was in a special bed hanging on the bulkhead in front of us. I was paranoid, knowing that even at this late date something could go wrong. I was sure that the man sitting next to me was from the Iraqi secret service, so I leaned over to Layla and whispered, "Don't say anything about us seeking asylum. As far as anyone is concerned, we're just tourists."

The plane flew to Copenhagen, from where we took an airport shuttle bus to the port. From there we caught the ferry to the Swedish seaport of Malmö. We planned to take a train from there to the city of Gothenburg, where my relative lived.

As we arrived at the Malmö train station, we met an Iraqi family that we learned had been with us on the plane from Baghdad. One of their relatives met them when they landed in Denmark and travelled with them the rest of the way. Overhearing their conversation on the shuttle, we noticed they were Assyrian Christians, like Layla.

Just before our train left, I struck up a conversation with the relative of the family.

"Hello, *Marhaba*." I said to him.

"Oh, hello." he replied, surprised. "Are you also Iraqis?"

"Yes we are." I replied.

I couldn't speak Assyrian, but to set him at ease, Layla started talking to him in his language.

Turning to me he asked in Arabic, "Where are you heading?"

"To Gothenburg."

"Really? That's where I live. Do you know anyone there?"

"Well," I admitted, "I know only one person—a distant relative."

"Who is he? I know a lot of people there; maybe I know him."

"Of course," I said, giving him the name.

"What a coincidence!" he said. "He's a friend of mine! You say you have his phone number?"

"Yes," I said, rummaging in my pocket to find a paper with his name and number. "Here it is." I showed him the number.

Glancing at the number, he said, "It's a good thing we talked. He got a new number just a few days ago. Shall I give it to you?"

"Yes, please," I said taking a piece of paper and jotting down the number.

What an unexpected encounter - and immediately on our arrival in Sweden! It felt like God was really looking out for us; we had known all along that we could trust him.

The train arrived in Gothenburg at eleven o'clock in the evening on Saturday, June 30, 1990. As we entered the train station hall, we were aghast at the sight: the station floor was covered with human bodies. At first, we thought something dreadful had happened to them, but we soon noticed that they were just asleep on the floor. In order to cross the concourse, we had to step over and between them.

"Maybe people in Europe are like that," I told Layla, hazarding a guess as to why they were there. "They must have the freedom to sleep where they want. What a liberal country!"

We found out later from a fruit seller that Madonna, the American rock star, was performing that day in Gothenburg, and people had converged from all over Sweden and Europe to attend the concert.

We tried phoning my relative, but nobody answered, so we continued trying to call him every hour until four in the morning. When we finally got through, we learned that he was just coming home from a party. He fetched us immediately and took us to his apartment. What a relief!

A few days after we arrived, we went to the police station, where we asked for humanitarian asylum. An officer there interviewed us and then sent us to the reception area, where we waited nervously.

After few minutes he returned, smiling, and said, "OK, you have been accepted as refugees and asylum seekers in Sweden. This does not mean you will be given permanent visas, but it does mean that your case will be taken up by the immigration office. They will make the final decision."

Wow, what a relief! Finally we had refugee status.

According to an international agreement, refugees must apply for asylum in the first country that will accept them after leaving their own country. Our translator told us later that the officer had phoned his boss to ask if we should be sent back to Denmark, since that was the first country we had entered after leaving Iraq. But the officer's boss told him to let us stay.

Our translator exclaimed, "Thank God—*alhamdulilah*. You are very lucky!"

The officer processed our papers and sent us on our way. Now it was time to go see our new home—a refugee camp.

22

REFUGEES

Refugee camp. It sounds worse than it really was. The camps were hotels and tourist facilities that were rented by the government. We lived in a spacious hotel room with adequate facilities, and shared three free meals each day with other refugees in the dining room. We were given a bit of pocket money as well. The camp staff treated us with courtesy and respect.

We thanked God that Sweden lavished this exceptional treatment on us. Finally we could relax. The tension and fear that had gripped us for so long gradually dissipated, although for seven years I had nightmares that I was back in the Iraqi army, fighting in the war. They only gradually diminished in the last two of the seven years and finally went away. But here no one was chasing me anymore. No one would again coerce me to fight.

Sweden is a country that is proud of its religious and political freedom. The Swedes have a great respect for human rights, freedom of speech, freedom of the press, and women's rights. The country is blessed with a very high standard of living and exudes a sense of peace and calm. Sweden is also blessed with incredible natural resources—forests, fields, mountains, lakes, and rivers. In winter, the white landscape is beautiful. The first time we saw snow, we were awed as we watched it fall peacefully to the ground.

It didn't take long, though, to learn that Sweden was not paradise on earth and also had its problems in spite of the beauty of its nature, the strong economy, and the excellent social services system.

Swedish social life seemed to us to be very individualistic, with little family cohesion and poor neighborly interaction. A Swedish pastor once told me that loneliness and estrangement were eroding society like a cancer, destroying family life, and feeding high rates of divorce and suicide.

Some Swedes were racist. Once as I was walking to a church to attend Swedish lessons, a car stopped by me, and four men sat looking at me. One of them opened the back door and started to harangue me. Of course, I couldn't understand him, but I was distraught by the way he yelled at me. Sometimes we would get dirty looks from people in stores or on the street.

An Iranian woman in our camp had fled her country because of the draconian laws requiring women to wear black clothing from head to toe in public. Now she was in despair over the racist attitudes in Sweden. She didn't fit into her own culture in Iran, and now she feared she would never fit into Swedish society either. She was so distraught that she became sick and had to be rushed to the hospital. I went with her in the ambulance, and when she arrived at the hospital she had a heart attack. Fortunately she recovered and when she was well, she invited us to her home for a sumptuous meal, including a delicious Iranian eggplant dish. Here we were, Iraqis and Iranians living in peace together.

Even among the various ethnic groups we saw this racial snobbery, and sadly, the churches were not immune.

So we were dismayed to see that, although most Swedes wished us well, there were some who resented our presence in their country. But I suppose we would have met this same attitude in most any Western country. Even in Iraq many people have a racist attitude toward the Egyptians, Sudanese, Chinese, and Koreans who work there.

A month after we arrived in Sweden we heard that Iraq had invaded its neighbor, Kuwait. So our fear that another war would break out was well founded! Thank God that we were in Sweden and not in Iraq!

The media began to report war tragedies, and we worried about our parents and relatives, as well as the Iraqi people. Of course, we were also worried about the poor Kuwaiti people, who were suffering under the attack.

Iraqis were again banned from leaving the country, making it difficult to avoid conscription and fallout from the war. Many deserted the army and fled the country, walking for days through the rugged mountains and snow to Turkey, or through the desert to Syria, experiencing all kinds of hardships.

Iraqi Radio proclaimed victory, saying that "the branch has been grafted back on the vine; our nations are now unified." My brother, Raad, who was in one of the armored units that entered Kuwait, said, "What kind of victory is this? I can see from the faces of the Kuwaiti people that they are angry and don't want this kind of 'unity'! This is not unification; this is occupation!"

On his first furlough from the army he deserted and fled the country.

After a year in refugee camps, we were awarded permanent resident status and moved to Gothenburg, where there was an Iraqi community, as well as a number of Middle Eastern churches. We settled on a church made up of Syriac Catholics, Maronites, Chaldeans, and Nestorians. The priest was a Syriac Catholic. Another reason for choosing to live in Gothenburg was that we were closer to the Chalmers University of Technology, where I intended to study, and the Catholic elementary school that our daughter attended.

One thing that struck us in Sweden was the embarrassingly large number of Christian denominations. Our desire was to fight for Christian unity, so we were sympathetic with the ecumenical church movement. Jesus has only one flock; consequently, Christians should not be divided. In addition to attending our church, we made the rounds of various Swedish churches in Gothenburg, regardless of their confession, to see what they were like: Catholic, Orthodox, Lutheran, Pentecostal, Baptist, and Evangelical. Many of these churches had few members, most of whom were elderly.

23

CHURCH LIFE

I began playing keyboard at Mass in our church, while Layla sang in the choir. I also began to play with several bands at clubs, celebrations, and parties. However, we became increasingly uneasy about the atmosphere at these functions. It was anything but pure.

Once I played in the Christian Assyrian social club. At the end of that evening, the club manager said that all the funds raised that evening were going to buy weapons for the Iraqi Christian soldiers in northern Iraq. That was quite a shock and wake-up call. What? Was I helping the war effort? I would not have any part in it! I discussed this with the other members of my band, but they didn't share my concern. In the end, I decided to quit playing at the parties and only play organ in the church.

We became aware of questionable practices that were going on right in the church. For instance, a young man who was a refugee without permanent residency, once came to church with a Swedish girl, and introduced her to us as his fiancée. We could see that she had emotional problems, so it was clear that he only wanted to marry her to get a visa. I went to the priest and protested, telling him he should not officiate at such a wedding, but he ignored my pleas and married them anyway. Several years later, we saw that poor woman processing a divorce application through the same church.

Unfortunately, these marriages of convenience were common, many people using this strategy to get permanent residency. Knowing the challenging circumstances that many refugees come from, it is difficult to judge, but still, this is a deceptive means to an end. Christians, especially, should never resort to such dishonesty. In the refugee camps we often heard things like, "Don't have a conscience crisis over it." "All that matters is to get a visa." "Get married, even if the woman is as old as your mother!" My brother, who sought asylum in Austria, refused to follow this path, even though he had to wait ten years before securing a permanent visa.

During this time we were studying Swedish in special courses for immigrants. To our surprise our teacher, Göran, was a committed Christian. As we got to know each other better, he started visiting us at home. We talked about Christian discipleship and what we needed to do to live for Christ.

He knew a lot of church history and shared with us about many groups we had never heard of. He told us about the history of movements like the Quakers, the Evangelicals, and the sixteenth-century Anabaptists. He also spoke about groups that were, or had been, active in Sweden: the Jesus Army, the Maranatha Community, the radical "wanderer priest" David Petander, and various Catholic movements.

Finally, he showed us a video about a group called the Bruderhof, a communal church of families and singles that try to live like the early Christians. He told us that members take vows of poverty, chastity, and obedience. There are no rich or poor among them, as they share all things in common, living a life of mutual service. They have a common source of livelihood, and their own private schools. They eat meals in common, and receive provisions according to their needs. Being a peace church, they practice nonviolence and do not hold political office. Family life and lifelong faithfulness in marriage are of utmost importance, so they demand complete purity before and outside of marriage.

We were quite impressed with their way of life. We were thankful that such groups as this existed and wished them God's blessing, although we never considered leaving our church to join them or any other group. We believed it would be a mortal sin for us to leave our church. Even so, we longed that all Christians break down the barriers that separate them in order to find unity in Christ, regardless of human labels. That was certainly what we wanted to work for.

24

WHAT IS CHURCH?

As Göran shared about the history of the church, he also warned us that there are false teachings in many groups. He showed us passages that diverged from the gospel in the publications of several groups.

Surprised, I started spending more time reading the Bible and Christian books to discover what was true and what was false. The church meant everything to me, so I was determined to know how Jesus intended her to be. But what a bewildering assortment of denominations and confessions there were! I began to ask the question, "What is the church?"

I knew that the early Christians were inspired by the Holy Spirit, but I soon learned that by the fourth century the church had devolved into an ecclesiastical institution, accepting many compromises. Church and state united when Emperor Constantine became a Christian and ended persecution against the church.

From that point on, the church was involved in politics and abandoned her stand on nonviolence. In fact, the military became so Christianized that by 416 non-Christians were forbidden to serve in the army.* Enemies of the Roman Empire became enemies of Christianity.

It is abundantly clear that differences between churches are usually over unimportant details such as rituals, prayers, and liturgies – not only in Sweden, but in many parts of the world. Unfortunately, when church services are over, it is difficult to distinguish between the lives of church-goers and the lives of non-believers. One crucial element that is missing is a fuller sharing of resources; individuals hoard their money and possessions with little thought of the needs either of brothers and sisters or the world at large. Each person has his own life and priorities. This is a result of a lack of a firm and lasting commitment to each other. The Christian's commitment to Jesus and his Church must take precedence over all other engagements, including marriage. Lifelong commitment can lead to deeper unity, a cure for many of the world's problems, common cause in the education of children, and a powerful witness to the truth of the Gospel.

Certainly, there are Christians who are deeply committed, but when it comes to sharing their lives completely with others, few are willing to take that step. And yet that was one of the most important, life-changing

---

* Cadoux, C. John, *The Early Christian Attitude to War: A Contribution to the History of Christian Ethics*, p. 589.

traits of the first church in Jerusalem.

I read in the Bible that the new believers in Jesus

> devoted themselves to the apostles' teaching and to fellow-
> ship, to the breaking of bread and to prayer. Everyone was
> filled with awe at the many wonders and signs performed by
> the apostles. All the believers were together and had every-
> thing in common. They sold property and possessions to
> give to anyone who had need. Every day they continued to
> meet together in the temple courts. They broke bread in
> their homes and ate together with glad and sincere
> hearts, praising God and enjoying the favor of all the people
> (Acts 2:42-47).

Well, it was clear from the Bible that the church should not only be a Sunday thing. The first Christians met together daily, and although they often met in the temple, much of their fellowship was in each other's homes— and they shared all their possessions in common. The churches I frequented certainly did not do that!

Jesus pointed out the difference between earthly rela- tionships and godly relationships. When someone told Jesus his family was waiting to see him, he told them, "Who is my mother, and who are my brothers?" He pointed to his disciples and said, "Here are my mother and my brothers. For whoever does the will of my Father in heaven is my brother and sister and mother" (Matt. 12:46-50). In other words, my real brothers and sisters— my real family—are those who share my faith, not neces- sarily those to whom I am related by blood.

The early Christians had a strong social conscience.

There were no rich and no poor in their midst, because they shared all their possessions in common. I was sad to see the stark differences in social and economic classes in the churches I attended.

One of the early Roman emperors complained that the Christians not only took care of their own poor, but they cared for the poor pagans as well. Yet, I saw little social conscience in Christian circles. Members were concerned about their personal salvation, but cared little for the temporal needs of those around them. The apostle James admonished the church with these words:

> What good is it, my brothers and sisters, if someone claims to have faith but has no deeds? Can such faith save them? Suppose a brother or a sister is without clothes and daily food. If one of you says to them, "Go in peace; keep warm and well fed," but does nothing about their physical needs, what good is it? In the same way, faith by itself, if it is not accompanied by action, is dead. (James 2:14-17)

Then there was the question of baptism. In the New Testament people were baptized on confession of faith. That is, adults who recognized their sinfulness and repented of their sins were immersed in water as a symbol of forgiveness. So why do many churches baptize infants? Don't children already belong to God's kingdom? After all, Jesus said, "Let the little children come to me, and do not hinder them, for the kingdom of God belongs to such as these. Truly I tell you, anyone who will not receive the kingdom of God like a little child will never enter it" (Luke 18:16-17). Jesus' disciples didn't baptize children;

they only baptized people who repented of their sin and confessed their faith in God.

Another important question was that of sin in the church. Too often pastors overlook the practices of parishioners that should be challenged: gossip, back-biting, impurity, and even outright immorality. It is true that some pastors do speak out, but there is no binding promise among the believers that allows them to confront one another. The apostle James urges us to hold brothers and sisters accountable for their actions when he says, "Whoever turns a sinner from the error of his way will save him from death and cover over a multi-tude of sins" (James 5:20).

The New Testament teaches us that anyone persisting in sin should be excluded from fellowship, and Hebrews 12:6 tells us, "For the Lord disciplines him whom he loves, and chastises every son whom he receives." If we truly love our brothers and sisters, we will do anything necessary to lead them back into fellowship through repentance. This sometimes requires a time of quiet withdrawal—what is called church discipline. This is in no way a punishment, but a time to reflect on what has gone wrong in order to find a new beginning. No church that I knew of practiced this.

Jesus was very clear about the sin of divorce and remarriage. He didn't mince his words when he said, "Whoever divorces his wife and marries another, commits adultery against her; and if she divorces her husband and marries another, she commits adultery" (Mark 10:11-12). Divorce and remarriage are simply not allowed in the church of Jesus Christ. I noticed, however, that there are many divorced and remarried people in the churches.

What about the church's involvement in politics, with its web of compromises and subterfuge? It seemed to me that Jesus was clear about the difference between the leaders of this world and leaders in his church. He said:

> You know that the rulers of the Gentiles lord it over them, and their great ones are tyrants over them. It will not be so among you; but whoever wishes to be great among you must be your servant, and whoever wishes to be first among you must be your slave; just as the Son of Man came not to be served but to serve, and to give his life a ransom for many. (Matt. 20: 25-28)

Jesus is saying that Christians should remain aloof from worldly politics. Their leadership is of a different order. Anyone, whether priest, deacon, or layman, who wants to serve in Christ's way must become a servant, not a boss.

All worldly governments, whether democratic or dictatorial, differ from the way of the church, which is characterized by unanimous agreement, particularly on important life issues of the gospel.

Although democracy is somewhat better than dictatorship, in the long run democracy also has serious drawbacks. In a dictatorship, a minority imposes its views on the majority, while in a democracy, the majority dictates to a minority. In both systems there is no total agreement. That is why, even in a democratic society, we see turmoil, inequality, and discontent.

The church has a different calling from that of worldly governments. God uses earthly governments to maintain law and order, and he uses the nations to judge the nations. So Christians do not deny the role of government in God's order; that is why they are commanded to respect those who hold temporal authority. But that is not the role of the church. This became clear to me after learning what the Christian's attitude to government should be when I read *God's Revolution*,* by Eberhard Arnold.

Finally, how can a Christian bear arms and participate in the armed forces? Aren't we commanded to love our enemies? How can we love them when we are killing them? The gospel of peace is in direct opposition to the warlike spirit. Having personally experienced war and the army in Iraq, I was especially sensitive to this last issue.

So I searched objectively for the truth and came to the conclusion that the church does not consist only of individuals who have been "saved," but must be a united community of believers who seek together, fighting for a new order of unity, purity, and peace. I was gripped by this conclusion because it spoke to the inner longing I had had for years.

---

* Plough Publishing House, 1997.

25

COMING TO CLARITY

With great excitement I began speaking to friends in our church about what I was learning. Some listened with interest, but most were indifferent. I hoped to inspire others to join me in seeking a life of total sharing, full devotion, and mutual daily service in an effort to transform the church from the inside out. Even most of those who were interested had reservations. Others disagreed outright, especially on the question of peace and the bearing of arms.

I once suggested to a couple of families that we all move to one area, where our children could play together, away from the questionable atmosphere on the streets. In this way we could raise and guide our children together, and we would have more time to spend with them. But no one responded, which disappointed me greatly. Most of our friends were too busy with their own personal lives and priorities.

Meanwhile in our church the various ethnic groups vied for recognition of their favorite saints. I had stopped playing music at parties and events some time before, but now I was so disgusted that I stopped playing in church as well.

I attempted to talk to our priest about Mary-worship, showing him sentences in a prayer book devoted to her such as "Worship is befitting her," and "Our salvation is in your hands." I told him that although I honored the Virgin Mary, adoration and worship should be reserved for God alone and his son, Jesus. I suggested we remove those sentences from the book. He said that he personally did not have the power to delete those sentences because the book was issued by the bishops.

While I struggled over the question of war and the bearing of arms, I decided to talk to our bishop in Gothenburg in order to get to the heart of the Catholic Church's position. I wanted to be perfectly clear about what the church taught, so I made an appointment and went to meet him personally. I told him about my experiences in the military and on the front lines during the Iran-Iraq war, and my resolve never to kill.

After hearing me out, he replied, "This may be your personal conviction, but the church takes a different stand." What the bishop said confirmed what I read in the *Catechism of the Catholic Church* regarding what is known as the "Just War Doctrine," first enunciated by Augustine.

Although the Vatican II council questioned the Just War theory in the mid-sixties, it went on to state that "as long as the danger of war remains, and there is no competent and sufficiently powerful authority at the international level, governments cannot be denied the right to legitimate defense once every means of peaceful settlement has been exhausted." *

We know how "Christian" countries fought in the two world wars. And every military base and warship has a chapel for the celebration of Mass and the Lord's Supper, as well as to provide spiritual counseling for personnel who will be going out to kill their fellow humans. The bishop tried to explain how the church's involvement in the military and politics is an attempt to have a positive impact on society. But I was not convinced by such rationalizations, which I found to be foreign to the way of Jesus.

At the end of my meeting with the bishop I concluded that, although the Catholic Church might compromise, I wouldn't. Hereafter, I would be compelled to take a firm stand on pure Christian pacifism, without compromising the clear commandments of Jesus.

I had a new, joyful determination to henceforth declare my conviction—even to governmental authorities, if necessary—that being a Christian means living

---

* Section 1, "The Avoidance of War. Chapter V, The Fostering of Peace and the Promotion of a Community of Nations." Pastoral Constitution: On the Church in the Modern World. *Gaudium et Spes.* Pope Paul VI, December 7, 1965.

and fighting for peace. I didn't want to spend another minute of my life serving things that undermined the cause of God's kingdom.

Now that the position of the Catholic Church was clear, I figured that belonging to a small flock that put all of Jesus' commands into practice was better than belonging to a church that would compromise the truth, even if it was the biggest church in the world.

I had at one time considered three possible ways to serve in my church. The first way was to become a priest. The second was to continue serving as a layman. The third was to join the Third Order of Brothers and Sisters of Mother Teresa in Sweden. But now I remembered what I had learned about the Bruderhof, a place where people not only lived a life of peace, but also practiced true community of goods. My heart was torn. I prayed that Jesus would guide me on the path he wanted me to follow. If we joined the Bruderhof our family would have to begin a new life in England.

I struggled over the question for several days, until I felt at peace. The answer was the Bruderhof. I had asked the Lord for guidance, and he had answered. Now, having been led by God to this decision, I felt it would have been a mortal sin not to follow through.

Before this decision to join the Bruderhof, I had hoped to resume studies at Chalmers University of Technology in Gothenburg to earn a master's degree in chemical engineering. Layla had also hoped to earn a diploma in accounting. But now we decided to simply respond to God's call and abandon these personal ambitions.

We got varying reactions from our friends and family, who thought we had gone completely nuts.

"What? Move to another country and join a cult? What are you thinking?"

"What's the matter with you? How on earth will you live without money or possessions?"

"How can you leave Sweden, with its high standard of living, and move to a community where you don't even have TV?"

As far as our friends were concerned, the Bruderhof community was just another little country village. They wondered why we needed to go there to live out our faith. "Can't you live your Christianity here in Gothenburg? Why do you need to move to a village in England?"

But this didn't bother us. We were very happy, because we had found the jewel of life—the pearl of great price. As Jesus said, "Again, the kingdom of heaven is like a merchant looking for fine pearls. When he found one of great value, he went away and sold everything he had and bought it" (Matt. 13:45-46).

I am convinced that there is a longing in the heart of every human being to live a life of brotherhood, free from unclarity and compromise. At least, Jesus had planted that desire in my heart. I give him all the credit, knowing that "he who began a good work in you will carry it on to completion until the day of Christ Jesus" (Phil. 1:6).

26

SEEKING COMMUNITY

At the beginning of 1993 we wrote a letter to the Darvell Community, in southern England. Although there are many Bruderhof communities throughout the world, Darvell was the closest to us at that time. We expressed our desire to join, and our willingness to leave Sweden, give up all our possessions, and devote our lives to the church. We didn't have Swedish citizenship yet–a security of us refugees–but we wanted to risk everything in order to meet the call of God, and go on his way, no matter what the results were.

The reply came, with a proposal that startled us: establish a small brotherly fellowship where we were in Sweden. Its core members would be my family and Göran. Our life would be based on the principle of full sharing, lifelong commitment, and submission to the teachings of Jesus. Darvell was getting a lot of visitors from Sweden, so we also thought that our little group might be a link between the Bruderhof and Swedes who were looking for a deeper walk with Jesus.

After spending a week in prayer, we wrote to Darvell saying that we took their suggestion seriously. At the same time, we hoped one day to be able to unite with them. Because we respected the Bruderhof, we did not want to establish a group for its own sake, but rather to seek unity.

We rented two apartments, one for our family and one for Göram and single guests. In an effort to lead a simpler life, we also gave away many of our material possessions. We wanted to conduct our lives with the same simplicity and modesty of dress as the members of the Bruderhof, and like their sisters, Layla began to wear a head covering.

In order to get our community started, we had to register as a charity and Free Church. We chose the name of *Kristen Brödra Gemenskap,* which means "Christian Brotherly Fellowship." We were legally permitted to teach our own children at home up until the age of six, so we started our own nursery school, to which some of our Swedish neighbors sent their children.

Since we needed some sort of common work, after much discussion and prayer, we decided to start a home bakery to sell pastries and cakes. Admittedly, this made me a bit nervous, as I'd never baked in my life, but we were doing this for the sake of Christ. It was worth getting our hands dirty. We bought a large oven and turned one of the rooms in our apartment into a bakery, so we could start selling baked goods to various local cafeterias.

We continued our involvement in many activities—Swedish Christian conferences, churches, Bible study circles. We also organized public meetings and conferences, some of which took several days. We offered food and lodging to overnight guests who participated in the conferences. From time to time, we had Swedish and Arab guests—both Christian and Muslim—for whom we also provided accommodation. Many who came to us wanted to follow the narrow way of Christ.

Every day we had meetings for prayer or Bible study or decision-making, and as we lived together, we grew together inwardly.

Our total income was less than the level of social welfare, but we didn't ask for aid. We wanted to earn our bread by the sweat of our brow. Incredibly, we made enough to give financial help to several needy people. God was giving us a lesson on faith, and we humbly and thankfully gave him the glory and honor.

About a month after we began, two brothers from the Bruderhof, who were visiting Swedish friends, paid us a visit. We hosted them throughout their time in Sweden, even helping them to organize a conference in our community.

Materialism, isolation, and individualism do not satisfy the inner longing of people wherever they are, whether in Europe or in the heart of Africa, so we were not surprised when people who were seeking new life came to us. Needless to say, the visit of these two brothers brought us a lot of joy. They were able to share about their life in Darvell, and the more they shared, the more eager we were to visit them in England.

In March of 1993 we were finally able to visit Darvell. Since our visit coincided with the Easter days, the room prepared for us was full of welcome cards and bouquets when we arrived. An elderly couple, John and Gwen, hosted us. They were very hospitable, treating us as though we were VIPs. Our hearts were stirred by the warm welcome and acceptance of people with whom we had no blood relation and who did not even know us.

We delighted in the simple life of work, meetings, and activities and experienced the joys and sorrows of the daily Bruderhof life, feeling heart to heart with the brothers and sisters.

The children are an integral part of the activities of the church community. They are simple, innocent, and peaceful and always greeted us with smiles. Although our English was far from perfect, we didn't feel any language barriers.

Elderly members are regarded with great reverence and respect and are given the utmost care. Single people are incorporated into families, so that no one is alone.

There is tremendous joy in the work, because everything is done for the cause of Christ and his kingdom. The brothers and sisters roll up their sleeves and dig into whatever tasks are assigned, without a lot of unnecessary talk.

In the community work is viewed as a gift from God, and I have to say, there is no end of work. Each brother and sister has a task. Some teach in the nursery school, primary school, or secondary school. Some prepare meals for the community, while others work in the laundry or in the offices. There is work in the maintenance department and the extensive farms and gardens.

Most people work at one time or another in the "shop," the Community Playthings factory, which produces furniture and play equipment for schools. This is the income-earning department that provides money for the daily needs of the community.

While working in the factory, I noticed that Jerry, a tall, blond brother, seemed to be in charge. I asked him once, "Are you responsible here?"

Smiling, he said, "Yes, I am the shop foreman." Then he added, humbly, "But I am really just one of the brothers. I run the shop only in a brotherly way."

Wow, that answer warmed my heart. After what I had experienced of leadership in the army and in the factory where I worked, it was comforting to know that there is a place in the world where those in charge do not lord it over the workers.

This reply was characteristic of the attitude of brothers and sisters toward leadership. They don't feel so much that they are "in charge" as that they are there to serve by helping to get the work done in an orderly way.

Reluctantly, we returned to our small community in Sweden, having learned a lot from the brothers and sisters in England. But on our return, life was not all roses. Having started our common life, the devil found ways to attack us and put obstacles in our way.

Gradually, over the next three years, we fell into a trap of asceticism. It took us a long time to realize that our desire for a simple life was leading to a spirit of stinginess and lovelessness. We became so frugal that we found it increasingly difficult to help others. Once we discussed for three days whether we should help one of my relatives, who went to Jordan with his family to escape the hell of Iraq. He needed financial support, but we argued over whether it was right to buy him razor blades, because we wore beards!

We also fell into the trap of religiosity—false piety and legalism. This trap is hard to describe and even harder to recognize. We began to lose our joy and delight in life: playing instruments, singing, dancing line dances, and fun activities, as well as our laughter and smiles. We refused to sing anything but hymns, as we wanted to sing only "for the Lord." We soon developed a boring, religious character, looking at the outward appearance of people and not taking into account the work of Jesus in the souls around us. Because of these problems, we began to lose touch with our friends—Christian, Muslim, Arab, and Swedish.

151

In the end, it became clear that we seemed to be heading in two different directions. Göran did not share our longing to join the Bruderhof. He was content to continue life as usual. So we challenged him that from the beginning we had planned to unite our group in Sweden with the Bruderhof, and we felt that now was the time to do it. Eventually, he agreed to bring our Swedish community to an end and move to Darvell with us.

We had had a rocky time together in Sweden, but would life in the Bruderhof be any smoother?

27

A NEW BEGINNING

In March 1996 we closed down our community and prepared to move to Darvell. The brothers and sisters warned us not to burn our bridges, because it often takes time for a new person to grow into a new community. This is compounded in the case of a family. People coming new to the Bruderhof need time to adjust, since the life is so radically different from life in the outside world. Often, those who come, thinking that they will stay, find after several weeks or months that they need a time of reflection before making the momentous step of committing themselves for life. So upon the advice of the community, we kept one apartment in Sweden in case we needed to return.

We travelled to Darvell in the spring and reveled in the joy and freedom we experienced as we threw ourselves into the communal activities. The frequent meetings were always arranged in a circle, with concentric rows of chairs—enough seats for up to two or three hundred brothers, sisters, and children, depending on the nature of the meeting. These gatherings were often lively, beginning with several songs that were called out spontaneously. A short exhortation would usually follow the singing, after which brothers and sisters had an opportunity to stand up and express what was on their hearts. These were deep times of sharing and seeking God's will, but even the deepest times were fraught with joy.

Although the community had a number of pastors, called Servants of the Word, they were never in the spotlight. In fact in our early days in the community we didn't even know who they were, as they lived just as simply as all the other brothers and sisters.

We often had fun evenings, with line or folk dances accompanied by a small band consisting of flutes, violins, acoustic guitars, bass, and piano. Sometimes we participated in communal games, plays, choir, and orchestra. The community fought against rigidity—anything that stifled love and creativity—and we saw the creative spirit at work everywhere we turned. New songs, artwork, and stories were regularly presented to the community for the enjoyment of all.

Once we were invited to the family of a Jewish-Christian brother, Josef Ben-Eliezer, who had had to flee the Nazi terror with his family when he was a child. He eventually found his way to Israel where he fought in the army during the Israeli war of independence.

Disgusted with the treatment of the Palestinians, he left Israel in search of brotherhood, finally ending up many years later in the Bruderhof.

I was shocked when Josef played a cassette of joyful Palestinian wedding songs for me. "But these are worldly songs," I said.

He was surprised by my unexpected comment but didn't say anything. I could see by the expression on his face that for him these songs were an innocent expression of joy. After giving this some thought, I realized that I can't make hard and fast rules about music, but must simply listen to the spirit of a song. Even classical music can have a negative side, so I learned not to look down on other styles of music or musical instrumentation. This was a balm for my soul, as I had long been involved in the music scene.

One important recognition for me was that brothers and sisters are often much more sensitive than I am to what needs to change in me. We often overlook our own faults, but in community we receive help not only to *see* these faults, but to *change*.

During one communal lunch, a group of young people came in, carrying a number of cakes decorated with cream. The people sitting at the tables watched, curiously, not knowing what was going to happen. Suddenly the young people shoved the cakes into the faces of select people. The whole dining room erupted in laughter. The cakes were not real—just shaving cream.

I was boiling inside, thinking that if anyone shoved a cake into my face, I would stand up and give him a piece of my mind. But gradually I began to see that I was full of religious pride. I was mortified at how easily I fell into religiosity. Over time, with the help of brothers and sisters, this critical spirit faded.

Some brothers noticed that my constant babbling was a disturbance; I was always spouting religious talk. One time we were invited to attend a meeting of young people who were seeking baptism, during which a couple of guests pumped the group with a lot of embarrassing questions. With self-assurance I fielded all questions, since the young people seemed to be hesitating.

The next day, Jesse, the brother in charge of the meeting, came humbly to me and said, "You know, Yacoub, the young people were disturbed yesterday by your attitude in the meeting when you answered all the questions."

I was surprised and asked, "What do you mean? I thought they would be thankful."

He said, "Well, the young people need to learn to think deeply and seek answers themselves, and we have to allow them to do that. But if we answer all the questions for them, we are holding them back by our human efforts." Then he gave some advice that I never forgot. He said, "Let the Spirit move."

That advice helped to strip the religious talk out of me. It also stripped away my confidence in my ability to convince others and win arguments using human reasoning. The truth is, only God can convict and change someone's heart.

I was ashamed of myself. It was a heavy blow, but necessary. From then on, I made an effort to be quiet and let the Spirit move and work in souls. Of course, this does not mean that we should never speak up or give advice. It means, rather, that we should learn to trust in the leading of the Holy Spirit, and wait for God's time to play our part.

Everywhere we went in the community we saw a poster labeled, "The Law of Love," or "The First Law in Sannerz." Looking at it closely, I was struck by the words:

There is no law but that of love. Love is joy in others. What then is anger at them? Passing on the joy that the presence of others brings us means words of love. Thus words of anger and worry about members of the brotherhood are out of the question. In Sannerz there must never be talk, either open or hidden, against a brother or a sister, against their individual characteristics—under no circumstances behind their back. Talking in one's own family is no exception to this either.

Without the commandment of silence there is no faithfulness and thus no community. The only possible way is direct address as the spontaneous brotherly service to the one whose weaknesses cause something in us to react negatively. The open word of direct address brings a deepening of friendship and it is not resented. Only when one does not find the way together immediately in this direct manner is it necessary to talk together with a third person whom one can trust to lead to a solution and uniting in the highest and deepest.

> Each one in the household should hang this admonition
> up at his place of work where he always has it before his eyes.

Eberhard Arnold, who founded the community in 1920 along with his wife, Emmy, in the little German village of Sannerz, had written this "First Law in Sannerz" after a crisis that nearly destroyed the community. Eberhard encouraged each household member to hang up a copy of this warning in his or her workplace, where they would have it continually before their eyes.

When I recalled the way groups and churches I had known were blown apart because of gossip, I marveled at this clear, insightful word. Brothers and sisters assured us that although they often failed, this "Law" always set them back on the right track.

28

EBERHARD

In those days we were expecting another baby and Layla was nearing her seventh month. We loved the name Faadi, which means "Redeemer" in Arabic and is a title for Christ. There was no name we loved more. On the other hand we thought we should consider names that make a radical Christian impact today. In the end we decided that if we had a girl, we would name her Emmy, but if we had a boy we would name him Eberhard. We chose these names thinking of Eberhard and Emmy Arnold who founded the Bruderhof movement.

On Friday, March 15, 1996, less than a month after our arrival in Darvell, we had to rush Layla to the hospital one morning because her blood pressure shot up dangerously.

A brother from the community drove us to the hospital, located near Hastings. When we got there, one of the doctors warned us that both mother and baby were at risk and there was a possibility that one or the other would not survive. There was no other option: Layla needed to undergo another caesarean section. We were devastated and both started weeping.

The operation took place that same afternoon, with a truly international team: an Egyptian doctor, English female nurses, and a Sudanese male nurse.

I was allowed to stay and support with Layla, who was partially anesthetized during the procedure. We were relieved to hear the baby cry soon after the birth.

"The baby is alive—alive! Thank God!"

One of the nurses told us, "Congratulations, you have a boy."

"Hurray, a boy this time!"

"What are you going to name him?" she asked.

"Eberhard," I replied. The nurses were surprised, since Eberhard is a German name and not very common in England. They whisked him off to the intensive care unit, because he was very tiny—only two and a half pounds.

Later in the evening, while I was standing by Layla's bed, she suddenly had a seizure. I was distraught and called to her: "Layla, Layla!" But she didn't respond. I ran to the nurses' station, and nurses came running to Layla's side. After a minute the seizures stopped, but Layla was unconscious.

The Sudanese male nurse explained to me in Arabic that these seizures, known as eclampsia, frequently accompany a pregnancy in women with high blood pressure. Following the seizure there is typically either a period of confusion or coma. He said that possible side effects were cerebral hemorrhage, kidney failure, or cardiac arrest. "We'll just have to wait and see if there are any complications," he warned.

All that time I was praying for Layla and the baby. The community supported us by sending brothers and sisters to stand with us during this difficult time. At one point a group, including our friend Josef, arrived. When I saw them I collapsed in tears, desperately worried. The seizures came and went, but finally stopped the next day, although Layla remained in a coma for three days.

Layla survived, miraculously, with no side effects or complications, but she and the baby had to remain for a month in the intensive care unit in Buchanan Hospital in St. Leonard-on-Sea.

During these weeks brothers ferried me back and forth to the hospital each day. Eberhard grew bigger and everything went well. One of the nurses said, "I have never seen such a beautiful baby before." He had blond hair and dark green eyes like Mariam.

But the nurse added, "No more babies—too dangerous!"

After that we had to take the baby to another hospital in Brighton for a month, where he underwent a hernia operation. Again, the community supported us during that time.

When we were finally united as a family at home in the community after these two harrowing months,

Lillian, a sister, was assigned to care for Eberhard during our first night, since we were so weary. He was a lively little chap, and kept her awake all night!

This painful experience was a wakeup call for me. For years I had used my "reasoning" to dominate Layla in order to convince her to agree with me. In fact it was largely because of my insistence that we had come to the community in the first place, not because Layla felt any particular calling. She followed my lead primarily to keep the family together.

Now, after nearly losing her, I began to see how hard-headed and controlling I had been. God was trying to use this experience to purge me of this attitude—like thrashing me with a stick to exorcise me of wrong spirits. It was painful but therapeutic.

29

REFLECTION

Living closely with brothers and sisters brings out both the best and the worst in us, so it is no surprise that during this time, the church could see areas where we needed to change. For one thing, in spite of all we had learned about ourselves, Layla and I were not united as a married couple and needed more time to find each other's hearts, so we could build a new relationship of love and trust.

Consequently, the church advised us to return to our home in Sweden and to give ourselves enough time to think about it quietly—also to give Layla time to heal and recover.

The return to Sweden was bittersweet. It was difficult to leave brothers and sisters and the life that we had grown to love so much. But we also knew that there was still much in us that needed to change. We left with a new determination to fight the demons in us, to find a new love and unity in our marriage, and to seek God's guidance. We knew we would someday return to the community when it was God's time.

I also knew I would have to give my wife the time she needed to come to this decision by herself, not because I had talked her into it.

It took six years.

Finally in the spring of 2002 we were completely united in our desire to return to the community. This time it was Layla who said, "Come on, let's get going! What are we doing here?"

So we asked the community if we could return.

Nearly all the musical instruments in the community were acoustic, so I was unsure how the community would react to my Arabic electronic keyboards. I hesitantly asked the brothers if I should bring them. "Sure, bring them!" I was told.

This answer pleased me. These people really did try to put Eberhard Arnold's words into practice: "There is no law but that of love."

We arrived back in Darvell on Saturday, July 13, 2002, and we thanked God that he had been patient with us, faithfully leading us during the last six years.

It was, of course, a joyful time as we reconnected with brothers and sisters who were now six years older. Some that we had known before were no longer living; others were new, having come from communities in other parts of the world. But we felt the same peace and unity, even from those we had just met.

Our children were also happy to be back. Mariam went into the eighth grade in the community school, while Eberhard went into first grade. Like the prodigal son, I felt like I had finally come to my senses and was returning to my true home.

On Sunday, the sixth of July 2003, we were baptized. By this time there was a second community in England, Beech Grove, located not far from Dover. Many members came from Beech Grove for the occasion. Brothers, sisters, and children gathered around the baptismal pool to witness our baptism.

As we looked around at the people sitting on the lawn and under the spreading branches of the trees surrounding the pool, we were struck by the way God had molded people from such varied backgrounds into a new whole. Josef Ben-Eliezer was the Jewish pastor who baptized us. The brothers and sisters looking on were British, American, Nigerian, German, Swiss, and Korean. Layla and I were Iraqi. On communities in other parts of the world there were brothers and sisters from Belgium, Paraguay, Puerto Rico, Morocco, Mexico, and Australia. And yet, we were one family, united in the peace and love of Jesus.

As Josef continued with the meeting, a white dove landed on the ground in our midst. All eyes were focused on the bird as it strutted all the way around the baptismal pool, then took flight—like a visible sign of the peace we found in this group of diverse people from many corners of the globe.

There were nine people in our baptism group. One by one, we came forward and recited the Apostles' Creed, then stepped into the water to be baptized. Layla and I recited the creed in Arabic. After all were baptized, we went over to a nearby lawn where all brothers and sisters stood in a big circle. We newly-baptized brothers and sisters went around and shook everyone's hands. I was elated as the brothers and sisters and children greeted me, and I began weeping for joy.

Don, another pastor in the line, looked lovingly into my eyes, which were streaming with tears. As he took my hand in his, he said with a smile, "Welcome home."

EPILOGUE

We have now been living in the Bruderhof for thirteen years, mostly in Darvell, but also in Beech Grove. We have also visited many communities in the United States and Germany. We thank God for everything we have learned through our life in Christian community. Our lives are very full and blessed. Helping one another and helping neighbors around our communities brings us joy.

Like all couples in our communities, Layla and I have had to turn to the church again and again for help in building up our relationship and finding healing during times of struggle. Thanks to our shared life, I have come to realize how rough my manner often is when interacting with brothers and sisters. I am slow of heart when it comes to caring for others, and often I am not sensitive towards the feelings, needs, and weaknesses of those around me. But my brothers and sisters help me to recognize these faults and help me to change.

One aspect of community that is important to me is the love of nature. Children naturally take great delight in nature and will spend many hours in the woods, running through fields of flowers, planting gardens, and caring for animals. In the community, children learn the names of birds, worms, insects, animals, and flowers. They help make compost, rain or shine. In the American communities they even learn to collect maple sap in winter and make syrup that is served in the community dining room. Being close to nature has had a calming effect on my soul and has encouraged in me a more childlike spirit and faith in God.

Like many Christians, I had spiritualized things so much that I was losing my love of nature. Seeing how close both children and adults in the community were to Mother Earth, my rigid attitude began to relax. I discovered that going to church was not the only way to praise God; I could also do it through the enjoyment of the huge, diverse creation that he made for me and all humankind.

The childlike spirit is very connected to music. Finding the right spirit in music takes discernment. If I can't sing a song or perform a piece of music in front of children, I shouldn't be performing it; there is something in it that will hurt the childlike spirit. This doesn't mean that the music has to be simplistic, because children are capable of enjoying music that is quite complex. But it must be offered in the right spirit. This is what we fight for in the community.

What unites us is the recognition that we are *all* sinners—fallible human beings in need of daily repentance, God's help and guidance, and his Holy Spirit. Jesus tells the story of the tax collector and the Pharisee:

> Two men went up to the temple to pray, one a Pharisee and the other a tax collector. The Pharisee stood by himself and prayed: "God, I thank you that I am not like other people—robbers, evildoers, adulterers—or even like this tax collector. I fast twice a week and give a tenth of all I get." But the tax collector stood at a distance. He would not even look up to heaven, but beat his breast and said, "God, have mercy on me, a sinner." I tell you that this man, rather than the other, went home justified before God. For all those who exalt themselves will be humbled, and those who humble themselves will be exalted. (Luke 18: 9-14)

This is a crucial recognition that leads to unity on the highest and deepest levels.

Of course, community life is not free of problems, and this is what makes it very real. Jesus calls weak people to be joined to him and we can draw strength and help from him, making brotherly sharing possible. As he promised: "I am the vine; you are the branches. If you remain in me and I in you, you will bear much fruit; apart from me you can do nothing" (John 15: 5).

Some months ago, Layla and I attended a humanitarian conference in Hastings, on the southern coast of England, several miles from Darvell. On the way home we took a taxi. We soon discovered that the taxi driver was originally from Iran, and we inevitably got to talking about the Iran-Iraq war. The driver listened intently, as I told him about my decision never to kill and that I would rather have let an Iranian soldier kill me than to harm anyone. When we arrived at our destination, the driver categorically refused to take any payment for the trip. Instead, he took me in his arms and held me to his chest for several seconds. Then, wishing me good luck, he went on his way. I was overwhelmed.

Indeed, Jesus' command to love even our enemies does bear fruit. Until the day I die I will be grateful to God for what he has taught me about the love of Jesus—a love that unites, reconciles, and heals.

FAMILY ALBUM

As a child

With my father

Aged 16

In the Army

Scene from Iran-Iraq war

Akhawiya Picnic

With my friends Hassan and Talib

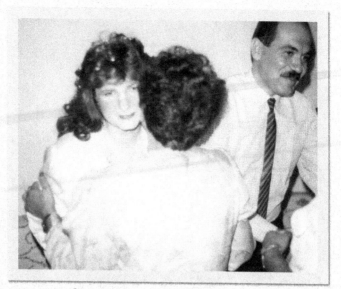

Layla and I during our engagement
My stepmother is greeting Layla.

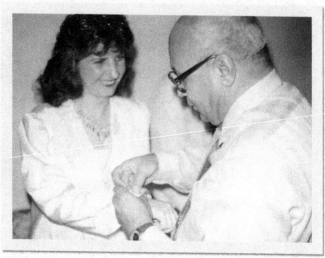

My father putting the gold jewelry on
Layla during our engagement.

Our wedding

Father Lucien Cup

Father Raphael Qtaimy with the Pope

*Celebrating our first Christmas
in the Al-Mashriq Club*

*Miriam's first birthday, celebrated in
the refugee camp in Sweden*

Mariam's infant baptism with Father Philip, relatives, and friends

Layla, Mariam and I with some friends of the Akhawiya in the yard of the Mar Ilia Al-Hiri Church, 1990

A jam session with some of the young men of the community. That's me on the drums.

Mariam and Eberhard making music in our Bruderhof home

We taught the community an Assyrian line dance during supper.

Visiting my mother in Germany

Our family living happily in the Bruderhof, ca. 2003

Communal picnic in Darvell

We went on a ponycart ride during our first visit to Darvell.

Layla and I by the shore in southern England, 2015